D0465209

The Teacher

The Teacher

D. Elton TRUEBLOOD

BROADMAN PRESS
Nashville, Tennessee

Dewey Decimal Classification: 248.4

Subject heading: CHRISTIAN LIFE//TEACHING//RETIREMENT

Library of Congress Catalog Card Number: 80-67088

Printed in the United States of America

Contents

Introduction   7

1. My Teachers   13
2. The Doctor   16
3. The New Teaching Role   19
4. The Habitual Vision of Greatness   23
5. The Strategy of a Minority   30
6. The Christian Intellectual   35
7. The Place of Theology in a University   45
8. The Minister's Study   58
9. The Love of the Difficult   67
10. Acropolis and Areopagus   73
11. The Self and the Community   79
12. Ethical Contagion   89
13. The Spiritual Dimension of Inflation   95
14. The Essential Christian Unit   99
15. The Wisdom of Paradox   103
16. The Jonestown Tragedy   107
17. What Time It Is   111
18. Life in Britain   115
19. The Middle East   119
20. Church and State   123
21. The Last Chapter of Life   128

Introduction

One of the secrets of retirement is to engage in it by degrees. If a life has had several different facets, one would be wise to conclude some activities while the individual is in full vigor; but it is not necessary to end all public activities at the same time. In my own experience, realizing that I had pursued the multiple vocations of teaching, writing, and speaking—and that these together constituted a ministry—I made the deliberate decision to reduce my work by stages. The part of my career which combines both writing and teaching has lasted the longest and is still enjoyable, even though I am now in my eightieth year.

In 1974, when I published my autobiography, *While It Is Day,* I made a firm decision to write no other books. That promise to myself has been kept; and, in order to avoid the danger of anticlimax, I shall continue to keep it. This promise did not, however, preclude the publication of previously printed essays in fresh collective form, with the hope of reaching new readers. One such collection, *The Encourager,* published in 1978, was made up exclusively of letters written in identical form, that of the periodical essay. Now, two years later, publication of a collection of fugitive essays has been undertaken at the instigation of Broadman Press. In the 1978 volume, all of the essays were *Quarterly Yoke Letters;* only the last nine of the present collection belong to this category. All of the other essays have appeared in other contexts.

The perceptive reader will notice that in the production of short essays, I have had a variety of models. The chief model is that provided early in the eighteenth century by Joseph Addison, who,

with others, originated *The Spectator. The Spectator,* the greatest
literary triumph of its time, succeeded partly because its purpose
was marked by unusual clarity. That purpose was "to cultivate
and polish human life, by promoting virtue and knowledge, and
by recommending whatsoever may be either useful or ornamental
to society." Because the essential human situation has not been
altered by changing technology, these aims, expressed in 1711, are
by no means obsolete now. All who seek to be conscious participants in the heritage of Joseph Addison are free to share in his
purpose, even though their means of accomplishment may differ
from his.

Because I have written a great deal, the essays available for
republication have been sufficiently numerous to allow the exercise of choice among them. I have sought to include only those
which seem to me to be both true and pertinent to our present
situation, as we approach the end of our century. Consequently,
most of the essays selected have been produced since my retirement from formal teaching. A conspicuous exception is the essay
"The Place of Theology in a University," which first appeared in
1942 when I was teaching at Stanford University. It is not surprising that several of the selected essays deal, in one way or another,
with academic themes. Recognizing the crisis in education, I am
determined to lift the level whenever and wherever I can.

The outcome of the process of selection is not a book, in the
strict sense of the term. If it were a book, there would be a
necessary sequence of the parts, the first chapter leading to the
second, the second to the third, and so on. There is not and cannot
be any such logical order of presentation here, though there is, to
some extent, the order of time. Even this, however, has not been
followed with any strictness. Consequently the essays can, without
loss, be read in any order which the reader may choose.

Very early in my life I began to realize that ideas were my chief
capital. In my teaching vocation I saw that thoughts are supremely precious—and that because they are precious, they must be

both preserved and shared. My chief means of preservation has been the constant use of a notebook or journal, while the most common means of sharing has been the essay. Personally, I value ideas so much that I sometimes get out of bed in the middle of the night to put fresh ones on paper, well aware of the fact that if I do not do so, the unrecorded thoughts may disappear forever. It has been helpful to realize that ideas can, without significant loss, be shared more than once. The fact that they have appeared in either a magazine or a quarterly letter does not mean that they cannot also appear between the covers of a book. Furthermore, the same thoughts can rightly be expressed in more than one context.

Though the written and the oral styles of communication are far from identical, the same themes can be adapted to both styles of discourse. A great deal of what I have written during the past fifty years has been spoken first. The notable advantage of this process is that, in their spoken form, ideas are subject to immediate response on the part of hearers. If an essay is given first as an address, the speaker has the immense advantage of the experimental method in trying to discern what is convincing and what is not, the faces of the listeners providing firsthand evidence of what the particular response may be. On the whole it is better to speak and then to write than it is to write and then to read aloud what has been written.

The title *The Teacher* was intended as a parallel to *The Rambler* and *The Idler* and has been chosen chiefly because the term designates the author's major vocation for more than a half-century. Acceptance of the appointment as professor of philosophy at Guilford College in 1927 established my life pattern, a pattern which I have tried to continue at Haverford, Stanford, Harvard, Earlham, and Mt. Holyoke.

When I retired from my professorship of philosophy in 1966, I could not foresee how rich and rewarding the new chapter in my life would become. I soon saw that my new career would include teaching, though performed in a different manner. Since giving up one kind of teaching only leaves the way open to others, it is a serious mistake to suppose that the joy of teaching necessarily ends with departure from the classroom and lecture hall. What has emerged is a new pattern in which most of my students are mature persons who come one at a time to my study, known as Teague Library, on the Earlham campus. Each student, of whatever age or occupation, begins where he or she is, and is encouraged to move forward as rapidly as possible. The informal pattern of Socrates is consciously emulated, including the elimination of any financial transaction of any kind.

The subjects of study have a wide range, the most common being logic, epistemology, and the philosophy of religion. The unregistered students are encouraged to bring or send the papers on which they are working. I try to read them carefully and to discuss them with the writers when they appear. Since good teaching includes both individual work and group support, the students involved in this new system are encouraged to gather with one another periodically in what we call the Socratic Society, for dining and sharing. In the dinners of the Society there are no set speeches, but each person is given a chance to report on work done or intended. A few of these new students have actually written and published books.

The climax of my postretirement teaching came, not in my own study and not in any American college or university, but on the Acropolis in Athens when I gave the lecture which is reproduced as chapter 10 of this volume. I found it a moving experience to be able to address 150 mature American students as they sat on the stones between the Parthenon and the Erectheum. At the conclusion of my lecture the students engaged in applause, but they were quickly hushed by the Greek guards, who reminded us that we were in a temple area.

Important as is oral discourse in the teacher's calling, this is by no means the only form which teaching takes. The teacher can operate by the written word, and ought to do so if he thinks he has something worth expressing. Recognizing this fact, I have employed much of my energy since my official retirement in written teaching on a variety of subjects. It pleases me to realize that I have numerous students who have never heard the sound of my voice. One of the concrete rewards which emerges in this kind of teaching is the reception of letters which otherwise unknown students voluntarily write, explaining where they stand in their personal studies and what their problems are. It is through this unsolicited correspondence that the intellectual dialogue becomes a reality., The daily arrival of the postman becomes an unscheduled academic event.

The price of sound teaching is high, for it comes only by constant discipline and by unending labor. Because the task is never really completed and the teacher is never fully ready, preparation until the last moment must always continue. Here Dr. Johnson's warning about Pope's lack of preparation for his *Essay on Man* is appropriate. "Pope," said Johnson, "was in haste to teach what he had not learned."

However arduous and demanding the role of the teacher may be, it includes many pleasures, chief among them being the joy of observing the development of other minds, as the potential becomes actual. The very term "teacher" has a long and honorable history. The Latin word *docere,* "to teach," provided us with the term "doctor"—the virtual limitation of the term "doctor" to the medical profession being a recent innovation. The conviction that teaching may rightly be viewed as a sacred calling is supported by the New Testament passage in which the "equipping" function is applied to both pastors and teachers (Eph. 4:11-12, RSV).

There is deep emotion in any contemplation of last things. As I have, perhaps for the last time, selected my scattered writings, I have been keenly conscious of companions on every side. These include my own teachers who have stimulated my mind; my students, known and unknown, with whom there has been a relationship of mutual assistance; and now you, my new readers, who

honor me with your thoughtful attention. Though my indebtedness is great and widespread, I am especially grateful, in connection with this new volume, to Mary Benson, whose secretarial skill
has enabled me to prepare the materials for publication.

D. E. T.

Earlham College
Pentecost, 1980

1
My Teachers

So far as is known, every one of my many teachers is now dead. Though I cannot, therefore, thank them today, I can at least express, in print, something of the magnitude of my indebtedness. Gratitude normally produces enrichment of life, particularly when teachers are involved, the bond between teacher and student having a unique spiritual character. I am grateful to many persons who have contributed to my pilgrimage, but I am doubly grateful to those who have brought enlargement to my life.

In my freshman year at Penn College I had the signal good fortune to be under the tutelage of a conscientious woman, Anna Eves, who required that I submit a six-hundred-word essay every Monday morning. Her patience in reading and correcting these amateurish efforts is almost beyond comprehension, but she never seemed to falter. She knew that the only way to learn to write is to write, and to keep at it everlastingly. Consequently, I soon developed the practice, maintained to this day, of never letting a week pass without engaging in some serious literary production. In heaven, I hope to visit Anna Eves as soon as possible.

My first Greek professor was that remarkable man, William E. Berry, who, like Anna Eves, taught first at Penn and later at Earlham. Greek was so difficult for me that I had to adopt the practice of rising at 5:00 AM in order to do my Greek composition before my 7:00 AM breakfast. Already it was obvious to me that prime tasks must be done in prime time. There were only five students in our Greek class, one of the brightest being Christina Hendry, later Mrs. Willard Jones, of the Ram Allah Mission in

Palestine. When we both settled in Richmond, Indiana, Dr. Berry and I became neighbors, always to my personal delight.

At Hartford Seminary, where I studied for one year, the greatest personal influence was that of Alexander C. Purdy, who quickly provided me a model, not only in his scholarship, but even more in his character and bearing. Our best times together came when we drove in his automobile every Sunday afternoon, between Woonsocket, Rhode Island, and Hartford, Connecticut.

At Harvard I soon came into close contact with Willard L. Sperry, who was both Dean of the Harvard Chapel and Dean of the Divinity School. I admired him as a famous Rhodes Scholar, as an athlete, and as a teacher. Before long he suggested that I write a paper for his scrutiny every week. He took his end of the arrangement as seriously as I took mine and did not hesitate to show me where I was wrong, particularly in pronunciation. For one entire semester we read together the long poems of William Wordsworth. He was the first to introduce me to the Christian classics of devotion. His favorite doctrine was that no person can be a really good writer unless he soaks himself consciously in a few great models. It was not wholly surprising that, ten years later, I wrote my first book on Dean Sperry's desk when, in the summer of 1935, I took his place in the Harvard Chapel.

Professor Oliver Elton, a visiting professor from England, influenced me in a different way. When he noticed that my Christian name was the same as his own surname, he went out of his way to be friendly. His advanced course called "Poetics" introduced me to the whole field of literary criticism and gave me my first serious start on both Plato and Aristotle. Before my acquaintance with Professor Elton I doubt if I had even heard of Longinus and I had not read anything of Horace. Toward the end of the course we were introduced to the works of Joseph Addison, Samuel Johnson, Coleridge, and many more. All of these I could have sought alone, but I doubt if ever I should have done so without the encouragement of a wise and good man.

The last and most demanding of my great teachers, the late Arthur O. Lovejoy of Johns Hopkins, was my mentor for three years in Baltimore and also during my first year of teaching at Haverford College. In his famous seminars he seemed, as one of his students said, like "Zeus on Olympus," the sworn enemy of all confusion of thought and the indefatigable champion of *clarity.* In spite of his dignified exterior I came to feel that he loved me. He still looks over my shoulder as I write.

Reprinted from *Quaker Life,* March 1979.

2
The Doctor

My connection with Woodbrooke, first as a student in 1924 and later as Fellow, in 1939, brought many blessings, eminent among them being the model of life provided by Dr. Rendel Harris. When I first reached Woodbrooke, the famous scholar was retired from his work with students in Selly Oak, but he was still a potent influence. We quickly learned the story of the venerable man, especially the part associated with Johns Hopkins University and Haverford College, before his return from America to become the first Director of Studies at the pioneering institution called Woodbrooke. He seemed to combine perfectly the culture of both parts of the Atlantic community.

Important as was his bond between Britain and America, Rendel Harris's career was even more significant in the union of the intellectual with the spiritual life. I suppose he was the first person I knew who combined perfectly keen rationality and unashamed piety. Though he knew and employed many languages and though he participated in the proceedings of learned societies, Dr. Harris was not ashamed to drop to his knees and pray like a little child. He saw no contradiction between childlike faith and adult intellectuality. In short, he came to illustrate for me what I later began to call the clear head and the warm heart.

My closest connection with "the Doctor," as he was invariably called, came in May 1939. By the good fortune of keeping a diary, I know exactly when we were last together. It was Whitsunday, May 28, and the place of meeting was the good man's garden in Birmingham. We talked especially of a connection dear to both of us, Johns Hopkins University. The old man was nearly blind, but his mind was as keen as ever. He spoke to me as "my dear boy," though I was thirty-eight years old, and I liked it.

In the midst of our final conversation, I asked Dr. Harris what was the secret of the undoubted intellectual renaissance at Hopkins in his time. "It was really very simple," he replied, "we all attended each other's lectures." Professor Harris listened to Dr. Osler on medicine, and Osler listened to Harris on ancient biblical manuscripts. "Wouldn't it raise your sights," he asked, "to have eminent scholars regularly in your audience?" I agreed that it would!

Long before I dreamed of a movement of Christian renewal, employing the biblical term Yokefellow, Rendel Harris stressed the central importance, in the gospel, of the famous Yoke Passage, Matthew 11:28-29. Dr. Harris began by quoting, " 'Come unto me, all ye that labour and are heavy laden, and I will give you rest. Take my yoke upon you, and learn of me; for I am meek and lowly in heart: and ye shall find rest unto your souls.' In the compass of these three verses we have the whole of the gospel message contracted within the limits of a single statement."

Perhaps someone had said this before; but, if so, I do not know who it was. The bold claim of Rendel Harris is that, in the invitation of Christ, we have the heart of the heart of the Christian faith. "There is no doubt," he said, "that this passage in Matthew not only has the gospel, but is the gospel." Deeply involved in biblical scholarship, aware of the problems of discovering the sources of the Synoptics, Harris could say, of the words of the yoke passage, "They have the ring of authenticity as no other words have."

Of all of the many writings of Rendel Harris, nothing equals those which perpetuate the messages given at Woodbrooke on Monday mornings. All of the students and teachers gathered reverently to pray together and to hear their beloved mentor. The modern reader can understand something of the high quality of the Monday morning addresses by noting how one of these began.

It is one of the distinctive features of Evangelical Religion to emphasize what is called the assurance of Faith, an experimental temper
which borders so closely on spiritual certainty, that the believer comes
to talk like a Gnostic, and faith appears to mark out for itself a claim
in the very area of knowledge.

It was not really surprising that when, in the Woodbrooke
Library, I wrote the text of my Swarthmore Lecture, *The Trustworthiness of Religious Experience*, I employed the sentence just
quoted as my opening epigraph. I employed it because Dr. Harris
had provided me solid ground on which to walk.

Reprinted from *Quaker Life*, November 1979.

3
The New Teaching Role

The more I think, and the more I mingle with committed Christians, the more clearly I become convinced of what it is that is now most needed. Wherever we turn, both within the Christian community and outside it, there is obvious need of instruction, in that people do not even know what the gospel is.

We have long noted the biblical illiteracy at every level of the populace, including those who have had academic opportunities. Because thousands of supposed Christians are unable to recognize any biblical quotation or allusion, there is consequent spiritual impoverishment. In some congregations the gospel has been diminished to the mere art of self-fulfillment. Some current religious authors, far from emphasizing what it means to believe that God was in Christ, reconciling the world unto himself, write chiefly of themselves. Egocentricity is all that is left when the objective truth about the revelation of Christ is lost or even obscured. In one recent religious book the pronoun "I" appears sixteen hundred times!

Part of the tragedy lies in the fact that, though seekers are, in many instances, prepared to hear a message of real magnitude, it is not provided for them by those who have the awesome responsibility of preaching to them. As we observe this mournful situation, we turn to the words of John Milton in his poem *Lycidas.* "The hungry sheep look up and are not fed." The fact that these immortal lines were written 340 years ago makes no difference at all because the truth of a proposition is never dependent upon the date at which it is uttered. We are simply experiencing a recurrence of a malady which has been suffered before and will be suffered again. The abandonment of basic Christianity is easy, having occurred many times in our history. That it appeared very early in the church is the point of departure of the apostle Paul in his letter to the Galatians. "I am astonished," he wrote, "to find you turning so quickly from him who called you by grace, and following a different gospel. Not that it is in fact another gospel; only there are persons who unsettle your minds by trying to distort the gospel of Christ" (Gal. 1:6-7).

What is most important for you and me is to realize that the spiritual desolation is both a challenge and an opportunity for the Christian who really believes something. The emptiness is so great and so evident that it determines, in large measure, the nature of our own task. Ours is a time when the gospel must be *taught.* Each one of us is now surrounded by vast numbers of women and men who constitute a genuine mission field. It is not that our neighbors have consciously rejected the gospel; they have never heard it! They do not really believe the tremendous news that God really *is,* that he is *like Christ,* and that *he has a vocation* for every son and daughter of earth. They have never been told that God is actually reaching out to everyone who is made in his image. They have heard of the Bible, but it is looked upon as obsolete literature rather than something that can speak to their condition here and now. They have heard the name of Christ, in profanity if in no other way, but it has never once been presented to their minds that he can be known in the present tense.

With an opportunity of such magnitude before it, the church of Jesus Christ must be redirected in its efforts and in its total ministry to the world. Those who guide the work of the church must know what the present need is and how to go about the task of meeting the need. Confusing as conduct may be, that is not the chief point of attack because the conduct arises from lack of convictions. The heart of the problem is what people believe or fail to believe, and this cannot be handled except by careful intellectual work, eventuating in sound teaching. There are, as the Scriptures say, many gifts, each of which is important; but different ones require emphasis at different times, depending upon the character of the dominant need. Once the need was that of social action, but times have changed. What is now most required is conviction about objective truth. If people do not believe that there are genuine values, they can have no answer to those who preach, "All is permitted."

Though the teaching ministry is what we must now emphasize, this is not new. When the word "pastor" is employed in the New Testament it is joined with the word "teacher" (Eph. 4:11). "Pastor" and "teacher" are not separated but constitute one category. The apostle Paul encouraged those who had the gift of teaching to employ it (Rom. 12:7). A pastor in the contemporary scene ought to visit the sick, but it is far more important that he should teach the seekers. The sorrowful truth is that, if he fails to do so, it probably will not be done at all. It may be true that no man is indispensable, but the good Christian teacher is nearly so.

As the church moves into the 1980s it must emphasize the teaching role. With the evident decay of the so-called Christian college which was founded to perform the role of teaching biblical religion, it is all the more important for the church to take over. Each pastor is potentially a teacher. I see every pastor as the dean of a little seminary, his own congregation and constituency. Every pastor who knows his business at all will be teaching courses.

If the church is to be worthy of its divine origin, it dare not stand still, but must always advance into new areas. In the recent past, we have made a significant step in stressing the "equipping ministry." That is still a sound emphasis, but now another new vision is required. What we must demonstrate now is a ministry which teaches because it helps people to *think*.

Only a sound teaching ministry can adequately motivate the

church to the fulfillment of all its divinely appointed ministries:
It takes the inner life of devotion, the outer life of service, and the
intellectual life of the mind. The Christian must learn to pray, to
serve, and to think. If he omits any of the three, he fails.

Reprinted from *The Herald,* September 1977.

4
The Habitual Vision
of Greatness

Long before he was a nationally famous man, Abraham Lincoln was asked what has been the most important invention of all mankind. With no hesitation came the answer, "The written word." The answer was, at the time, a surprising one; but its correctness is obvious when we think carefully about the question. No mechanical invention, however ingenious, can equal the process by means of which the human mind is enabled to bridge the chasms of both time and space.

The chief wonder of the written word lies in the fact that it permits a finite human being to choose his companions. Since the invention of the written word, whether on stone, clay tablets, or paper, anyone who can understand the meaning of curious marks is no longer limited to his own age or his own place of abode. The word is really the tremendous liberator, one of the means by which we become free.

It is a very exciting idea to realize that a person living in the twentieth century can, if he will, become really familiar with the thinking of Plato, the most famous of all writing philosophers, who wrote his dialogues in the fourth century BC. Indeed, the modern seeker even has an advantage over most of Plato's own students in the Athenian Academy because most of them never saw several of the famous dialogues, whereas we can read all of them.

In a similar and even more important way, the modern Christian can have more knowledge of Christ which was not available to his first followers, who became his disciples before they realized who he was. The paradox is that we have an advantage over those who conversed with our Lord by the Sea of Galilee because we have the four Gospels and they did not. Only later did the demand for knowledge of Jesus Christ, particularly on the part of Gentile Christians, lead to the production of books telling of what Christ did, what he said, how he died, and how he arose. We recognize, when we think about it, that several of the apostles died too soon to have our own inestimable advantage.

While the written word provides every literate person with incalculable wealth, there is a special way in which it enriches any minister of the gospel who is willing to take advantage of what is offered. The minister has the responsibility and privilege of providing wisdom about life to those who hear his voice, but the product in human lives depends almost entirely on the quality of experience which the speaker represents. He cannot give what he does not have!

If the thinking just presented is correct, there are few tasks more significant for the growth of the kingdom of Christ than that of the minister's choice of reading. It is perfectly clear that the wells have to be filled if expendable water is to be available. As the body becomes, in large measure, what the person eats, so the mind of the minister is influenced by what is perused and by the thinking which ensues. Out of the inner springs the rivers rise.

Even after we are aware of the importance of the written word, we still encounter serious temptations. One of these is the overemployment of television. Some televised programs are undoubtedly excellent, but the inferior ones far outnumber the valuable ones. The danger is indiscriminate viewing, which leads to one of the worst of sins, the waste of God's gift of time. Here the famous words of William Penn are applicable, though they were penned almost three hundred years ago. "There is nothing," wrote Penn, "of which we are apt to be so *lavish* as of time, and about which we ought to be more *solicitous;* since without it we can do nothing in this world. *Time* is what we *want most,* but what, alas! we *use worst;* and for which God will certainly most strictly reckon with us, when time shall be no more."

One of the evils of television, which seems to be intrinsic, is its essential passivity. The person before the screen merely *looks;* he is audience *par excellence.* There is no text on which he can write his reactions, expressing the growth of his own consequent thinking. With a book, however, there is abundant opportunity to write in the margins, between the lines, and in the blank spaces at the end. A book in which a person does not write is not really his own, and this applies to the Holy Scriptures as well as to other writings.

Whoever invented and promulgated the fad of rapid reading has done us a signal disservice. Anything that can be read rapidly is not worth reading in the first place! One of the best situations in which a person really grows is that in which he reads a good book, stopping frequently to record his own reactions either in the book itself or on other paper. The making of one's own index on the blank end pages of a good book is a really productive practice, partly because it saves sacred time in hunting through the entire volume to find prized passages. The fact that a book already presents an index, made by the author, does not relieve the thoughtful reader from the responsibility of making his own.

Probably the worst mistake a minister can make in his reading is to limit himself to strictly contemporary productions. There are many people who, when they pick up a book, look first at the date, meaning to discard or neglect it if it is old. This is a particularly stupid practice because it would, if consistently followed, lead to nothing but superficiality. Indeed, if a person is forced to choose between the new and the old, the part of wisdom is to choose the old. This follows from the simple fact that the old books now available have survived the sifting process of human experience, while the strictly contemporary ones have not. The vast majority of books published today are absolutely worthless. It is highly probable that a few will prove valuable, and will, therefore, survive; but the number surviving is bound to be small. It is an important step in wisdom to realize that the truth of a proposition is never dependent upon the time it is uttered. This is why classics are possible. It is absurd to refuse to learn from *The Imitation of Christ* simply because the book was produced five hundred years ago. The very fact that it has endured so long ought to encourage a thoughtful person to study it with particular care. Careful readers of Boswell's *Life of Dr. Samuel Johnson* will not easily forget the famous sage's comment on this very point, made in 1778. The book, Johnson observed, "must be a good book, as the world has opened its arms to receive it."

On the whole a minister will be a better representative of Christ in the world if he or she pays close attention to the wisdom of the late Alfred North Whitehead, who said, "Moral education is impossible apart from the habitual vision of greatness." The individual minister may realize, humbly, that he is not great, but this need not keep him from walking with the great. In fact, the more modest a person realizes that he is, the more he needs the contact with greatness which the written word makes everywhere possible. The wonderful effect of immersing one's mind in really great writers, rather than trashy ones, is that something of their character wears off on the reader. The humble man becomes, in part, what the giant whom he tries to emulate already is.

Of all the reading of the minister, no volumes are more important than the classics of devotion. Fortunately, they are easily available, though many Christians do not really know one of them. A wise minister will introduce these to those under his spiritual care, but he must first know them himself. Of those that are really indispensable, the following stand out clearly:

> *The Confessions of St. Augustine*
> *The Little Flowers of St. Francis*
> *The Imitation of Christ*
> *The Private Devotions of Lancelot Andrewes*
> *The Devotions of John Donne*

The Pensées of Blaise Pascal
A Serious Call to a Devout and Holy Life, by William Law
The Journal of John Woolman
The Christian's Secret of a Happy Life, by Hannah Whitall
    Smith
Testament of Devotion, by Thomas Kelly

There are a few others besides these ten, but any minister who allows the books mentioned to be part of his experience day after day will actually experience something of "the habitual vision" of which Whitehead spoke so eloquently.

One happy result of immersion in the recognized classics is that a minister's own devotional life may grow accordingly. As he reads the great journals of the spiritual giants, he may be encouraged to keep a journal himself, recording faithfully the growth of his own mind. Also, as he studies the written prayers of those whom he admires, he may see the wisdom of writing his own prayers. These may not be intended for any eyes other than his own, but that does not constitute a problem. The very exercise in honesty which the writing of personal prayers entails may finally make a difference in a person's public work.

Since the name of Dr. Samuel Johnson has already been mentioned in this essay, it is appropriate to introduce his practice of writing prayers for crucial occasions. Among these are the prayer in beginning Volume II of the famous *Dictionary,* when the toil of the days ahead appeared to be almost unbearable. This prayer is so short, so honest, and so applicable to the lives of most readers that it may profitably be memorized.

> *O God, who hast hitherto supported me, enable me to proceed in this labour, and in the whole task of my present state; that when I shall render up, at the last day, an account of the talent committed to me, I may receive pardon, for the sake of Jesus Christ. Amen.*

The contemporary minister of the gospel is not likely to be writing a dictionary of the English language, but he will have problems as real to him as were the problems of the famous lexicographer. The particular prayer of Dr. Johnson was written April 3, 1753. He noted that he was leaving room for Preface, Grammar, and History, "none of them yet begun." No wonder he felt the need of God's aid. Boswell, when the two volumes were finally completed in 1755, said, "The world contemplated with wonder so stupendous a work achieved by one man, while other countries had thought such undertakings fit only for whole academies."

Nearly every life has periods of stress, when the tasks contemplated seem to be too great to be done and the burdens too great to be borne. In such circumstances the great models can be helpful to persons such as ourselves. It is never enough to read the noble passages passively; they are not really honored unless we make some consequent productions of our own.

Nearly all ministers suffer from the fullness of their personal lives. There is something about their vocation which causes them always to try to schedule too many events. The result is that they become hectic and driven. There are far too many meetings, and the church is the worst of all sinners in this regard. Every good minister has a great many demands upon his time, his energy, and his emotional reserves. There is no way in which he can meet all of the requirements, most of which arise from human need.

The time a minister spends in attention to the miracle of the written word is not time taken from his central task, but, instead, time which makes his central task possible. Every good person is tempted to suppose that he ought always to be available in the effort to solve personal problems. The difficulty, however, is that the springs go dry. A person who is always available is not worth enough when he *is* available. Even our Lord left the people on the plain, when they needed him, to go apart to the mountain. It is wrong to stay always on the mountain, but it is equally wrong to stay always on the plain. The minister who learns to hide, partly to engage in the deepening of his own life through devotional reading, is a better man when he is not hidden.

5
The Strategy
of a Minority

The longer I live the more truly I am convinced that events are a commentary upon the Bible, even more than the Bible is a commentary upon events. It seems to me that in my lifetime I have seen many developments that make the words of the Bible come alive. For example, in the dread days just prior to the Second World War, the book of Revelation came to mean much more to me when I knew something of what went on in concentration camps, in the strategy of terror, and in the consequent development of a secret underground movement. Nero suddenly seemed modern because modern men were Neronic.

Now we are in a time different from that of the Second World War, yet in some ways equally disturbing. We are in a time that is especially hard for anyone who seeks to be a faithful Christian. Never in my life have I known a time when the attacks on the gospel were as vicious as they are now. I see about me a far more militant atheism than I have ever known, and I see it pressed with evangelistic fervor. I recognize that some of the most damaging attacks on the validity of the gospel are coming from those who claim some kind of marginal connection with Christianity. I see a widespread impersonalism that is frankly based on the idea that Christ was wrong in addressing the heavenly Father as "Thou."

At the same time that I note these vicious onslaughts and hear them almost every day, I also am aware of an exceptional vitality in the Christian cause at certain specific points. I see a marked growth in the concept and practice of the lay ministry. I see a development in the direction of reality of membership. According to this, in a few congregations, it is beginning to be expected that every member should participate seriously in the Christian cause, engaging in witness, in financial sacrifice, in daily ministry, and in study. There are, indeed, a few churches in which a small number undertake to conduct a highly demanding experiment for a limited period of time, with the thought that it may become continuous after a trial period.

Another great thing I see is the acceptance, on the part of some, that the Christian faith cannot be genuine unless it includes both the inner life of devotion and the outer life of service. A good many now realize that inner devotion can be self-centered or even self-indulgent, while mere service can become sterile and superficial. It is good to know that some can see that social protest without a tender and moving spirit is essentially self-contradictory. In short, in the brightest spots in the Christian cause it is truly understood that the roots and fruits of the Christian faith must be held together in one context. Many of the far-out people reject prayer and engage only in what they call "action." Others so emphasize prayer that they have no energy left for action. The hopeful spots are those in which people see that prayer and action are two sides of the same Christian coin.

When I think of the attacks upon Christianity and the small groups that represent great vitality, I have a better insight than ever before into the great biblical passage of 1 Corinthians 16:9, "A wide door for effective work has opened to me, and there are many adversaries" (RSV). What this text says has always been true of the Christian cause, but the events of our time make the truth unusually evident.

It is well known that we usually need to say more than one thing in order to tell the truth because the truth is essentially complex. This is especially the case when we talk about the prospects for the Christian faith. The coming years will be dark times and they will be bright times, and they will be both at once.

One of the most important things to say about the Christian

movement in the time immediately before us is that Christianity is bound to be a minority movement. It is important that we should know this because any failure to know our true situation will be bound to lead to weakness. As Lincoln taught us, we are more likely to know what to do if we know where we are and whither we are tending. Nothing makes for weakness more than does optimism or complacency when the conditions do not sustain it.

The superficial judgment of most of our people is to the effect that Christianity is strong in our country. This judgment is based upon the number of church buildings and the number of members on the church rolls. We do not need to have very much experience, however, to know that this strength is nothing like as great as it appears to be. Vast numbers who call themselves Christians are not participants in the ongoing work at all. Most are not regular in prayer or Bible reading or do not think of themselves as called upon to minister for Christ and their fellowmen. It is also important to see that the majority of persons in any large city quite evidently think that what goes on in the churches is truly irrelevant to their lives. There is more open ridicule now than there has been for many years. The characteristic faculty members in characteristic universities are openly contemptuous of anyone who takes the gospel seriously. The general idea is that those who do so are back numbers.

If Christians can know that they are in a minority, they will be better prepared to take their right places in the struggles of the coming days. They can be helped by remembering that the most glorious periods of the Christian faith have often been those in which the faith has had a minority status. This is conspicuously true of the Christianity of the New Testament period, which has, in many ways, never been equaled. If we know that we are surrounded by many enemies, we are far more able to understand the words of 2 Timothy 2:3, "Take your share of suffering as a good soldier of Jesus Christ" (TLB). Our great call is a call not to popularity or to ease but to loyalty in the face of persecution. It is important to know that there can be real persecution, even without physical violence. There are many places, especially in the intellectual life of America, in which it takes real courage to stand up as a loyal follower of Jesus Christ.

I do not mean that Christians should get out and wave banners and draw attention to themselves. One makes his Christian witness not by drawing attention to himself or by censorious and self-righteous judgment of others, but by the humble and unostentatious firmness of one who tries to do a decent job in the ordinary world and to put as much as he can of the spirit of Christ into his daily conduct.

As we honestly face our minority status, we shall soon learn that we have to carry on Christian work in new ways, or at least in ways new to *us*. I believe we shall carry on for a long time the Sunday morning gathering of the Christian forces, and for this I am glad, since it is better than nothing. But my prediction is that other expressions of Christian life and thought will tend to be relatively more important. It may be helpful to try to state what these are.

One is the increased use of the printed word. Churches have long had libraries, but only a minority have had regular book tables presided over by informed persons who make the spread of good books a genuine ministry. I think we shall see a significant growth of this particular form of Christian ministry. The sad truth is that most people do not know how to buy books and very few ever order them. The only practical alternative, therefore, is to put books where people are almost forced to encounter them. They must be made to understand that ownership is important because it permits both marking and lending to others. The really vital congregations will be those in which the characteristic members build up excellent libraries. Only by such an operation will they be able to have answers to those who challenge them about the hope that is in them.

Important as book tables in church buildings may be, they will never be sufficient because great numbers of those who need the ideas represented in the books will never darken the doors of the church buildings. Therefore, the Christian book service must be taken to the places where the people are. Perhaps these will be airports, perhaps shopping centers. A Christian book center in a busy airport in which people are often forced to spend unexpected hours may become a far more effective way of penetrating the world than is the conventional building on the corner with the pointed windows and the doors locked on weekdays. In any case, the Christianity that is effective in the coming time will be the Christianity that can learn imaginative ways of making its message understood.

An ideal setup, which we are already beginning to see in a few places, is that of combination lounge and bookstore. It is a combination of a Christian Science Reading Room and a commercial bookstore minus any denominational label or intent. Many will respond in a situation in which books *can* be purchased but need not be. Those who do not wish to buy anything may sit and read, wholly without embarrassment, while for those who want to buy there will be the possibility of frankly commercial transactions.

There will, of course, be a good many Christians who will try to proceed with business as usual, as though there were no cultural storm; but their effectiveness will be less and less. The effectiveness will be shown by those who, on the one hand, are firmly rooted in a living connection with the living Christ, but who, on the other hand, are not willing to keep this experience to themselves. The novelty, which is important, will lie not in the field of theology but in the field of effective witness. There is enough of this already to make ours a time of greatness.

Reprinted with permission from *Christianity Today,* February 4, 1966.

6
The Christian
Intellectual

The words with which Charles Dickens began *A Tale of Two Cities* were meant to apply to the period of the French Revolution, but they apply equally now, for the famous opening, "It was the best of times; it was the worst of times," has an astonishingly contemporary ring. Fantastic successes in some areas of human experience are now balanced by radical failures in others. Sometimes both the success and the failure appear in the same individual life.

The paradox of the greatness and the littleness of humanity to which Pascal gave brilliant expression more than three hundred years ago is now demonstrated for all to see. The greatness is especially obvious in technology. Not all believe that we should have used our energies to put a man on the moon, but no one can fail to be impressed by the skill required. Yet, at the same time, the despair in millions of minds is equally striking.

A quarter of a century ago a few of us began to say that faith in the possibility of a cut-flower civilization is a faith which is bound to fail. What we meant was that it is impossible to sustain certain elements of human dignity, once these have been severed from their cultural roots. The sorrowful fact is that, while the cut flowers seem to go on living and may even exhibit some brightness for a while, they cannot do so permanently, for they will eventually wither and be discarded.

The historical truth is that the chief sources of the concepts of the dignity of the individual and equality before the law are found in the biblical heritage. Apart from the fundamental convictions of that heritage, symbolized by the idea that every person is made in the image of God, there is no adequate reason for accepting the concepts mentioned. Since human beings are often far from admirable in their actual behavior, their dignity is fundamentally derivative in nature.

Always humans have broken laws; that is nothing new. What is new is the acceptance of a creed to the effect that there really is no objective truth about what human conduct ought to be. The new position is not merely that the old laws do not apply, but rather that *any* moral law is limited to subjective reference.

While this has been the position of a few individuals in the past, now this has suddenly become the position of millions. Some of them still have a slight connection with the Judeo-Christian heritage, but even that will finally dissolve if the obvious conflict in convictions continues.

If there is no objective right, then there is not even the possibility of error, and intellectual and moral confusion are bound to ensue. The most frightening aspect of this situation is the degree to which it renders the masses vulnerable to some new dogmatism which may arise. This will not be Hitlerism, since that has been fully discredited; but something like it may again succeed if the people have nothing better than their own subjective whims to oppose to the new creed. After all, Hitler had his own "thing."

As we analyze our moral situation, noting that the new permissiveness is becoming ever more fashionable, we must understand that the consequent predicament is not a simple one. Part of the oddity is that many people who, on one side of their lives, conclude that there is no moral order to which they owe allegiance as human beings, still retain some capacity for moral outrage.

Most protests are couched in terms of moral indignation, though they are sometimes made by people who claim to reject all moral requirements in their own lives. Theoretical moral indifference is coupled with actual, absolute moral condemnation of others. If we were consistent this would not be the case; but we are not consistent. Some who reject any possibility of objective reference in moral judgments are still shocked by murder.

Probably we ought to look upon this inconsistency as a sign of hope, indicating that people may be better in their personal conduct than in their philosophy. The taxi driver who boasts that he will do anything to get ahead, and that he has no moral principles, may in practice be scrupulous about his reading of the meter even when the passenger cannot see it.

The greatest single benefit to our contemporary civilization may come, not from some new invention, but from the reinvigoration of the roots which have, at various periods, produced cultural flowers almost universally admired. Though these roots have been shamefully neglected, they are not dead; and with sufficient thought they may be made productive again. At least, since there is a chance of success, we are driven to the effort by the revelation of the unsatisfactory character of all known alternatives. Millions now assume, without argument, that the biblical view of life is obsolete; but it is conceivable that they are wrong. It is my deepest conviction that they *are* wrong!

We hear, repeatedly, the cliché that deeds are everything while beliefs are unimportant; but this is manifest nonsense. Belief leads to action, and acting often depends upon believing. We are wise to remind ourselves of what Dr. Johnson said to Boswell on July 14, 1763, apropos of a man who denied the existence of a moral order: "If he does really think that there is no distinction between virtue and vice, why, Sir, when he leaves our house, let us count our spoons." If men believe that slaves are not fully human they will treat them as they treat animals. A man who is convinced that something is impossible will not, if he is intelligent, try to produce it.

Unfortunately, the intellectual effort that modern man so desperately needs, especially in his faith, is not being generally encouraged. Instead, there is a real discouragement produced by the preaching of anti-intellectualism. What we hear and read, over and over, is that the existence of God cannot be proved. The consequence is that many draw the erroneous conclusion that all items of faith are devoid of intellectual support. Since men certainly will not seek what they are convinced they cannot have, the effort to develop a reasoned faith is naturally not even attempted.

However bad some arid intellectualism has been, anti-intellectualism is worse, since it provides no antidote to either superstition or wishful thinking. If the tough-minded concern for evidence and for consistency is given up, there is no way to detect error, or even to distinguish between degrees of probability.

It is now widely recognized that absolute proof is something which the human being does not and cannot have. This follows necessarily from the twin fact that deductive reasoning cannot have certainty about its premises and that inductive reasoning cannot have certainty about its conclusions.

The notion that, in natural science, we have both certainty and absolute proof is simply one of the superstitions of our age. We have, of course, high probability, but that is a different matter. Even in the first great burst of scientific reasoning, in what Alfred North Whitehead called "the century of genius," it was already recognized that absolute proof is not given to finite minds.

Thus Blaise Pascal asked his fellow scientists, "Who has demonstrated that there will be a tomorrow, and that we shall die?" (*Pensées,* no. 252.) He knew that all science depends upon assumptions which are incapable of proof.

Once we face honestly the fact that complete demonstration is not within our scope, we are in a far better situation to do what we *can* do. Whether we are considering the existence of God or the existence of atoms, we need not, because we lack certainty, give up the effort to *believe honestly,* for though nothing is supported perfectly, some items of faith are far better supported than others.

The greatest danger that comes from frequent repetition of the phrase "God cannot be proved" is that it lodges in the public mind the idea that reason has nothing to do with the matter at all. This leads millions to the impotence of mere "fideism." The word means acceptance of "faith alone," with no concern for intellectual content.

The crucial difficulty of this position, however popular it may be at times, is that it provides no means of *choosing between* radically different faiths. It gives no basis for rejecting the Nazi faith or even the faith of voodooism. Once the life of reason is rejected, there is no reason why any one faith is better or worse than any other. People who say they do not need to give reasons for the objective validity of the faith they espouse do not seem to realize how sad the consequences of their position are.

The current rejection of apologetics is both misguided and futile, for it abandons the citadel to the enemy. Even the harshest critic of basic Christianity has no objection to the affirmation of a faith which cannot defend itself before thoughtful minds, since he can afford to be tolerant of anything so weak, because he is fundamentally contemptuous.

Accordingly, one of the most urgent tasks of contemporary Christians is to express a faith which can be made credible for modern humanity.

Enthusiasm is not enough! It will do something for a while, but it will soon evaporate unless the faith which is espoused can be stated so that those who do not share the enthusiasm can be convinced in their minds. No faith can survive unless it meets the double tests of intellectual validity and social relevance.

Few tasks are more important for Christians now than that of a reconsideration of the function of reason. We need to try to understand what reason can do and what it cannot. One of the most brilliant observations of Plato concerned what he called "misology," which he said was the worst thing that can happen to a man. The misologist is a person who, having become discouraged by his inability in dialectics, concludes that careful reasoning has no value. By this step he succeeds in transferring the blame from himself and his own ineptitude; but he undermines, at the same time, any possibility of detecting error. "Let us then, in the first place," said Plato, "be careful of allowing or of admitting into our souls the notion that there is no health or soundness in any arguments at all" (Plato, *Phaedo,* 90E).

Though reason is necessary to the Christian faith, it is probable that most people are not, in fact, drawn to a full faith by intellectual arguments. While the late T. S. Eliot was so drawn, it must be admitted that he was exceptional. "Can you by searching find out God?" (Job 11:7) is still a question to which the answer is presumably negative.

But if we end at this point we are missing important elements of practical significance. One of the chief of these is that strict honesty in reasoning may help immensely in answering objections to the faith that is centered in Jesus Christ. Though reason alone may not enable men to find God, it can do wonders in enabling them to surmount serious barriers to the achievement of an examined faith.

A graduate student in a leading American university asked one of his philosophy professors, who was not a Christian, whether his studies in philosophy would help him to see the truth of his Christian faith. The professor, after answering that these studies would not have this effect, added, "Your studies will do something that is equally important. They will enable you to answer the attacks upon the faith. Your opponents are more vulnerable than you or they realize."

The way to be a nonconformist today is to revive the heritage of "obstinate rationality" presented by Socrates. This can be especially powerful if it is joined by the use of humor, including the ability to laugh at oneself and one's own pretensions. Though the tough use of reason does not assure attainment of all of the answers, it at least makes us aware of questions not otherwise raised. Reason does not make us wholly free from mistakes, but it is wonderfully effective in making us *detect* the mistakes we make.

As we try to find our way through the confusion of a period in which many are convinced that there is no dependable point of trust, it is helpful to recognize our middle position as finite minds. We are equally separated from absolute certainty about the truth and from absolute ignorance of it.

Pascal clarified our middle state when he wrote, "Now there is, humanly speaking, no certainty, but we have reason" (*Pensées,* No. 822). Part of our dignity lies in the fact that we can be aware of our necessary humility. Though no belief about the world is entirely demonstrable, the claim that we have nothing on which to depend is not a logical consequence of our fallibility.

The more rational we become, the more we are concerned for the objectivity of truth. The same proposition cannot be true for one man and false for another, because then the confusion would be intrinsic and the effort to know the truth would be a meaningless undertaking. Here the clarification provided by Alec Vidler is particularly helpful. Speaking of the Christian faith, Vidler has written, "Either it is true for all men, whether they know it or not; or it is true for no one, not even for those people who are under the illusion that it is true" (Alec Vidler, *Christian Belief,* p. 10).

Though the subjective judgment of any individual man or group of men may be mistaken, it is essential to the life of reason to recognize that there is something which the individual or the group is mistaken *about.* What men are mistaken about is what we mean when we refer to the truth, regardless of the character of the inquiry. What we must do, as finite persons, is to try to improve our methods of inquiry so that, whether we are speaking of atoms or of the living God, we can be brought progressively closer to knowing what is, in distinction to what we happen to desire. "I prefer to believe" is an unchristian sentence.

The recognition that the function of reason is largely involved in the comparison of difficulties is one of the major steps in philosophical thinking. Though the idea applies to the whole of philosophy, the thinkers of the twentieth century who have expressed it most eloquently are both theologians. These are H. G. Wood of the University of Birmingham and John Baillie of the University of Edinburgh. Both men reported the immense intellectual relief which they experienced when they realized that it is not wise to give up a position when it seems to involve difficulties, unless it is possible to find an alternative position that exhibits less serious difficulties.

There are, for example, serious difficulties associated with the conviction that there is life after death, some of them having to do with the problem of how consciousness is possible subsequent to the physical decay of the brain. But a person of any intellectual maturity is also aware that there are equally serious or even greater difficulties attending the conviction that the death of the flesh is the end of the human story. The point is that it is unduly simplistic to reject any position without a careful examination of its alternatives. Serious as are the problems of Christian belief, the problems of unbelief may be even more serious.

When the enemies of reason seek allies they frequently quote the familiar words of Pascal, "The heart has its reasons, which reason does not know" (*Pensées,* no. 277), but in this they are making a serious mistake. Pascal, himself an unusually keen rationalist, is not their ally. When he contrasts the reasons of the heart with the reasons of the head he is not denying reason, but instead is seeking to show the necessity of the involvement of the entire person.

In saying that reason, as ordinarily understood, is not all there is, he is not denying but rather supplementing it. "We know truth," he said, "not only by the reason, but also by the heart" (*Pensées,* no. 282). Pascal would have been the last man to make a defense of unreason or to encourage misology.

In T. S. Eliot's examination of Pascal's method we find something of a model of what the procedure of the Christian intellectual should be. Pascal, says Eliot, looks at as much of the world as he can see and proceeds by rejection and elimination. He finds in the world as observed that which is inexplicable on a nontheistic basis and proceeds to a conclusion, not as a dogmatist, but as an intelligent seeker trying to make sense of his world. "Now Pascal's method," wrote Eliot, "is the method natural and right for the Christian" (T. S. Eliot, *Pascal's Pensées*, p. xii).

In this I heartily concur. Pascal has become our teacher because he was explaining to himself the sequence that culminated in his vital faith. He was not, regardless of the proposed name of his book, the public apologist, but primarily the reporter.

What we desperately need is the literature of witness in which men who have reached a firm place to stand are able to tell us the road by which they have come and why it was taken. We need a whole new group of thinkers who are willing and able to obey the injunction of 1 Peter 3:15, being prepared to make a defense of the "hope that is in them," but doing it "with gentleness and reverence." The result may be that the word apology will lose its present connotations.

Finally we are witnessing the verification of Whitehead's prediction of failure in the midst of advance. "The dawn of brilliant epochs," he said, "is shadowed by the massive obscurantism of human nature" (Alfred North Whitehead, *The Function of Reason*, p. 43). Once, large sections of the clergy were the standard examples of obscurantism, but today their places have been taken by the academic philosophers. Whatever else academic philosophy may do in our generation, it is improbable that it will provide desperate men and women with a firm place to stand in the face of the present confusion and perplexity about values.

Indeed, the forfeiture of values is one of the saddest elements in the plight of the big universities, and the departments of philosophy must bear a large measure of responsibility for this development. The intellectuals we need will necessarily stand in the heritage of Socrates and Pascal rather than in that of Protagoras and Montaigne.

A major problem is how basic Christianity can be presented as a live option for our troubled time without seeming to run off an old record which people will dismiss because they suppose it is familiar. Actually, of course, there are millions for whom it is not familiar, but this they do not know.

We are not likely to get many of these people, who are the most characteristic of our time, to read the New Testament because the dogma of its irrelevance to their problems is unquestioned. What is conceivable, however, is that a good many may be open to an approach which stresses logical thinking. Even an elementary acquaintance with the new mathematics provides an understanding of the process of implication. Having long supposed that religion is merely a matter of emotion, some may be pleasantly surprised to face a basic proposition, along with its major implications.

The key to the logic of belief lies in finding a firm place from which to operate. Since the necessity of such a starting point has long been recognized in both mathematics and science, it is reasonable that the same should be true in dealing with the questions that affect human life most deeply. Every set of logically connected propositions leads us back finally to some primitive proposition.

The primary proposition for the Christian, his ultimate act of faith, is *the trustworthiness of Jesus Christ.* It is here that the Christian finds a fulcrum that is firm.

Reprinted from *Christian Life,* March 1969. Portions of this essay have been printed in Chapter 1 of D. Elton Trueblood's *A Place to Stand* (New York: Harper & Row, © Copyright 1969), and are used by permission.

7
The Place of Theology in a University

The place assigned to theology is one important index to any culture. We know something significant about the early culture of America when we realize that, so far as academic life was concerned, theology occupied the focal point. We likewise know something important about the culture of the recent past when we realize that the place of theology has been the precise opposite of its former position. In the average institution of higher learning, theological studies have in recent times been banned, minimized, or barely tolerated. Thus we have vibrated between two extremes, but in our day there is appearing a great eagerness to find some conception of the place of theology more fruitful than either of these extremes has been. The first stage of our history in this regard was that of *Theology Dominant,* the second that of *Theology Excluded,* and the third may be that of *Theology Respected.* The purpose of this paper is to explore briefly the third possibility.

I

Since the exclusion of theology is still the major practice in our modern universities, we must try to understand the reasons for this exclusion. These reasons are essentially two: first, the conviction that theology is not worthy of academic attention, and second, the fear of sectarian teaching.

(1) The first of these two reasons is that of convinced naturalists, positivists, and secularists who are possibly in the majority at the present time, so far as our university faculties are concerned. They are aware that the world has had many theologians, but they

believe that these scholars have not produced anything worthy of critical attention. In Newman's excellent phrase, they believe "that the province of Religion is very barren of real knowledge."

What can a theologian teach? Is he not talking merely about his own speculations, speculations on which there is no possible objective check? If persons teach mathematics their conclusions are either right or wrong; if they teach physics their experiments either succeed or fail; if they are engineers their machines either run or don't run. But when a person discusses the knowledge of God, is he not merely using big words to express his own subjective ideas and emotions?

Some of these objectors to theology as an academic discipline are fundamentally antagonistic, not only to theology but to all religion. Religion, they hold, is something which really intelligent people already have outgrown and which everyone eventually will outgrow as they become fully critical. Religion, in short, is *superstition,* and there is no more reason why a university should teach this particular superstition than that it should teach astrology or palmistry. A university is, to be sure, a place of universal knowledge, but there is no requirement to teach what is outmoded.

Other objectors consider themselves friendly to religion while they have no intellectual respect for theology. Many are tolerant of religion and even attend places of worship on great occasions, but they do not see what religion has to do with *knowledge.* Religion seems to them to be a matter of the emotions and aspirations or ideals, sometimes misguided, but for the most part beneficent. Such emotions and ideals are all right in their place, but they have no valid connection with an advanced educational enterprise.

(2) The second reason for excluding theology is the fear of sectarianism. Parents may desire the omission of theological studies because they do not want the minds of their children contaminated by what seems to them dangerous thought. Thus there are devout parents who deliberately send their children to a state

university because they fear the dangerous religious instruction of other institutions.

An excellent example of how devout motives may lead to the elimination of theology is provided by the will of Sir Josiah Mason, who founded what is now the University of Birmingham. As H. G. Wood, the first professor of theology at Birmingham, has shown, Sir Josiah Mason specifically excluded theology, not because he had a positivistic contempt for religion but because, being a devout man, he feared sectarian controversy as much as he feared political controversy. It is this fear of sectarianism which is the dominant consideration in the thought of many administrators of state universities. *What* theology, they ask, will be taught? Will it be Catholic, Protestant, or what? Will it be modernist or fundamentalist? Will not our Catholic citizens raise a storm of protest if we use tax money to pay a Protestant theologian, and vice versa? Some of the independent universities have been as fearful of sectarianism as the state universities have been. Thus the founding grant of Stanford, while it provided for positive teaching concerning the existence of God and the immortality of the soul, declared that the university should never be the scene of sectarian teaching.

Similar to the fear of sectarianism is the fear of ecclesiastical domination. Many have in mind periods of our history when some church used great pressure and limited freedom of intellectual inquiry. The story of the supposed warfare between science and religion is still uppermost in many academic minds, even though this story has no bearing on contemporary experience. The church which is most feared in this connection is the Roman Catholic Church.

Finally, there are numerous administrators and professors who suppose that theological studies in tax-supported institutions are strictly illegal. This illegality seems to them to follow from the principle of separation of church and state.

II

Impressive as these objections to the inclusion of theology in a university curriculum may be, any objections are really beside the point, inasmuch as theology is not *actually* excluded in any academic situation. We cannot avoid the subject even when we try. When we try to avoid it, as is done in some institutions, what we get is an amateurish theology which is often not even recognized as theology at all. There are many universities which, though they deliberately exclude religion for fear of sectarian indoctrination, give a completely free hand to those who wish to indocrinate their students in naturalism. The religion of secularism comes in as a substitute in countless cases when the knowledge of God is eliminated. "I observe," wrote Newman, "that if you drop any science out of the circle of knowledge, you cannot keep its place vacant for it: that science is forgotten: the other sciences close up, or, in other words, they exceed their proper bounds and intrude where they have no right."

We have numerous sad illustrations in our time of the way in which a spiritual vacuum does not remain empty. Indeed this seems to be one of the major facts in regard to the cultural life of central Europe. With the manifest weakening of the Christian forces, the young people have become easy marks for new and fanatical faiths which are often old faiths in new garments, some so old as to be wholly barbaric. *The house that is swept and garnished cannot remain empty.* Even in America something similar, though not so drastic, can be abundantly illustrated, and would be worse under critical conditions. It is a sad commentary on our university life to notice the degree to which our young people become the victims of religious faddists. Though our students have built up, in their literary and scientific experience, some standards of judgment so that they are able to distinguish between that which is profound and that which is superficial or narrow, the same students have no such standards in their religious life. Com-

ing to the teaching of Jesus, for example, with the naïveté of the
wholly illiterate, they tend to take the teaching of the first exposi-
tor who meets them, with entire gullibility. A civilization in which
even educated people have not built up any standards by which
to judge new Messiahs is a civilization which is in great danger.

Even if the teaching of theology *could* be avoided it ought not
to be avoided, because of the vast importance and interest of the
subject. Here Newman's reasoning of ninety years ago is still
unanswerable: "A university, I should lay down, by its very name
professes to teach universal knowledge: Theology is surely a
branch of knowledge: how then is it possible to profess all
branches of knowledge, and yet to exclude not the meanest, nor
the narrowest of the number?" The effort to arrive at some knowledge of God is one of the oldest of human enterprises and is
manifestly not trivial in its purpose, whatever it may be in its
results. How curious to seek disciplined knowledge about the
world, but neglect the disciplined knowledge of its Author.

If we seek to get all of the knowledge and especially all of the
relevant knowledge we can, it would seem obvious that we ought
to seek especially for any knowledge of God. How exciting such
knowledge would be if it could be at all genuine! It is interesting
to know whether there is an atmosphere on the moon, but such
a question does not greatly affect our practical lives. The question
of the reality and nature of God, however, affects our lives in the
most intimate way. If it is true that we are not alone; if our own
feeble efforts are backed up and supported by the power that made
the world; if, to use Montague's phrase, what is "highest in value
is deepest in nature"; and if we could really know this with the
same degree of certainty which we have in regard to our knowledge of trivial things, life would suddenly become radiant and
glorious. The importance of this subject should make educators
unusually careful not to miss anything which might conceivably
be discovered. The very claim which religious knowledge puts
forward is itself so ambitious, however humble the scholar may be,

that no educator, wishing to introduce his students to as much of
the nature of reality as possible, could carelessly avoid any possibility of fruitfulness of approach.

III

The two objections that are raised against the inclusion of
theology in a university are not only beside the point; they can be
answered with great definiteness in the light of recent thought and
experience. In the first place, those who would exclude theology
on the ground that it is barren of real knowledge are merely
illustrating a fashionable academic prejudice. They are wholly
ignorant of the degree of sophistication which contemporary
theology involves. They do not know that numerous theologians
accept the same standards of trustworthiness in evidence which
competent natural scientists accept. They do not understand the
degree to which their own beliefs, scientific or otherwise, rest on
the same epistemological bases as does the knowledge of God.
They assume that religious experience is wholly subjective because
it is experienced in the minds of men, but they do not realize that
the same argument would deny objectivity to all their own data.
In short, they are ignorant and unscientific, not having open
minds on the subject. They are still fighting old battles, still referring to times when the church supposedly limited freedom of
scientific inquiry, unaware that the shoe is now on the other foot.
Moreover, they seem to have forgotten, if they ever knew it, that
the Christian faith is the mother of colleges.

In the second place, the omission of theology from a university
because of fear of sectarianism has practically no contemporary
justification, so long as we are dealing with men of university
caliber. One of the most revealing of the facts which bears on this
question is the difficulty of knowing the denominational background of many of the men who come to speak before university
audiences. Many of the great universities invite, as visiting preachers, men of national reputation; and more than one university

president has pointed out his difficulty in distinguishing between them on a sectarian basis. As one president remarked, they all say the same thing whether they call themselves Methodists, Baptists, Quakers, or Jews. The same could be added for many Catholics and representatives of other groups. A most practical approach to this problem would be provided by an actual test of the ability of cultivated people to distinguish between the denominational backgrounds of various leaders. The strong likelihood is that they would not have any conspicuous success in this regard, provided that the men speaking were men of the highest academic discipline.

The nature of the discipline is, of course, the crux of the matter. If the men who speak and teach are as well trained in their field as other scholars are in theirs, they will be as little sectarian as the scientists are. The real divisions in the modern religious world are horizontal rather than vertical. Almost every Christian has the illuminating experience of finding that there are great numbers in other denominations with whom he has far more in common than he has with most of those in his own. On the part of those who have given most attention to the subject, there is today a keen sense of what is fundamental in our Judeo-Christian message, a real catholicity of spirit and teaching. Insofar as we draw our leaders and teachers from this group, we shall find that sectarianism is a nonexistent boogey man.

When we speak of the discipline which is required of such men, we must remember that method in academic experience is quite as important as information. A good administrator, choosing a scientific professor, is not so much concerned with the professor's encyclopedic knowledge as he is with the discipline of his mentality, which will make him trustworthy in experimentation and research. The man with the right method can get the information if the information is available. All of us in the modern world have some appreciation of scientific method—and with good reason, since it has produced marked, tangible results—but students of the

humanities have been unduly impressed with scientific method
and consequently have exhibited undue modesty about their own
approach to the truth. There is a method different from scientific
method, but parallel to it, which is both difficult to learn and
fruitful when learned. This method is not as easy to describe as
scientific method is, but we can easily point to men who have
obviously learned it and who have the same reason to be trusted
in regard to the spiritual life which various great scientists have
to be trusted in regard to their investigations of physical nature.
The popular notion seems to be that, whereas it takes great and
precise training in order to be a scientist, one man's opinion is as
good as another's when we consider questions about the nature of
God and man and the history of ideas. The discipline required in
the humanities and divinity is not easier, but harder than that
required in most branches of science, because it deals far more
with probabilities, in which there is no rule of thumb and no
quantitative measurement. The major qualification, in short, is the
disciplined sensitivity of the observer, who cannot fall back on
crucial experiments for support.

Here we have a situation similar to that in the very highest
branches of science, where only the expert can be trusted. An
important task of the future is the more careful description of
what the appropriate discipline of the theologian really is. Professor Lovejoy has made some approach to this in his studies in the
history of ideas, and the Archbishop of Canterbury has made a
bold attempt at such description in his distinguished Gifford Lectures, especially in the chapter, "Logic, Mathematics, and History." What the Archbishop is attempting to do is to describe a
method which is as applicable to his field of interest as mathematics is to the field of interest of the natural scientist. The very fact
that this important task of description is still in its formative stages
is one excellent reason why theology should be studied in a university. This is the kind of question with which those who are dedicated to the advancement of learning should be vitally concerned.

The truth is that universities can find disciplined men who rise above sectarianism, and this takes care of the legal requirement in most states. Even the California law, which is one of the most strict in the separation of church and state, does not forbid the teaching of religion, but only the *sectarian* teaching of religion. Inasmuch as our Western civilization is so largely founded on Christian principles, it is not sectarianism to deal with these principles in an objective manner. Why should it be sectarian to discuss Saint Paul and not sectarian to discuss Hitler, who is certainly the leader of a religion now? The fact that various state universities carry on religious teaching with no legal difficulty is an important piece of evidence. This is possible because men are appointed who accept the same standards of probity in research, whatever their denominational affiliations.

IV

Considerations such as those just mentioned have led to a number of pioneering efforts in the reintroduction of an important discipline into our academic experience. Evidence of the widespread reopening of the subject may be found both in the institutions originally devoted to theological education and in those originally antagonistic to such education. At about the same time, Princeton University and the University of Birmingham established new professorships, Princeton appointing George F. Thomas "Professor of Religious Thought" and Birmingham appointing H. G. Wood the first "Professor of Theology." Both of these scholars produced inaugural lectures of great clarity and persuasiveness, interpreting their new tasks for a wide public. Professor Thomas's address is published as "Religion in an Age of Secularism" and Professor Wood's as "The Function of a Department of Theology in a Modern University." The former has been widely discussed in this country, and the latter would be if it were better known. The task of the one was to revive something that had almost ceased to be, and the task of the other was to

inaugurate something that had never been. In the trust deed of Sir
Josiah Mason, previously mentioned, it is "provided always that
no lectures or teaching or examination shall be permitted in the
institution upon theology or any question or subject purely theological." New regulations and the gift of Edward Cadbury have
effected a complete reversal of this situation.

Other evidences of a new interest in the subject are the publication of *The Case for Theology in a University,* by William Adams
Brown, the addresses at the Bicentennial Conference of the University of Pennsylvania, and the discussions on both coasts insti-
gated by the Hazen Foundation. Paul J. Braisted, the Program
Secretary of the Hazen Foundation, has published recently a pam-
phlet "Religion in Higher Education" which has been sent to the
presidents of all institutions of higher learning in the nation. Con-
siderable prominence has been given the fact that several state
universities, of which Oregon is a conspicuous example, have
well-established professorships in religious studies. What once
seemed a closed question is now conspicuously open.

V

If theology must be included in a university, to whom should
it be taught? *Chiefly to the faculty.* They are the ones who need
it most and the ones who, being well instructed, can have the
greatest influence. They cannot avoid theological implications and
even direct references to theological matters, but these references
are often woefully amateurish.

It is our duty to instruct professors in those subjects concerning
which they are bound to speak and yet in which they are manifestly ignorant. The greatest harm comes from the flippant, smart
remarks about religion from professors who may be educated in
their own lines, but who are wholly ignorant religiously. Many are
still fighting the old battles of their own youth, judging the Christian religion by some feeble, small-town church and worrying
about old struggles between science and religion. How tired

Galileo must be of being mentioned! In short, they are not up to date. Often they know nothing of the teaching of modern men like Reinhold Niebuhr and William Temple and would be surprised to know of the intellectual integrity of such persons. The fact that they speak out of ignorance does not mean that their remarks do no harm. It is well known that one of the ways in which a professor, ambitious for popularity, can get a laugh is by making remarks which are supposed to shock his students or at least to shock the more pious among them. This easy road to popularity is taken by many, but with a terrible price. The students who are very young and tender begin to suppose that there is something laughable about faith in God. Humor is a potent weapon, and the right use of this weapon can only be made possible by educating the men who use it. We ought to carry on theological seminars for the faculty and bring in men who make it their special task to do this kind of advanced teaching. In my own university we recently made a modest beginning in this regard by the use of William Adams Brown and with so much success that we hope to expand the practice in the future.

VI

Though the chief teaching of theology should be directed at faculty members, some should be directed at students, and we must decide how this is to be done. Our best insight is that religion should be taught in a religious way, just as science should be taught in a scientific way. The religious opinions of the irreligious are not more worthy of attention than are the scientific opinions of the unscientific.

Examples of the irreligious teaching of religion are abundant. Courses about religion are sometimes given in psychology or anthropology, courses which make the initial assumption that religion is simply a function of human nature and that divine revelation may be neglected without loss. To teach this as the truth is, of course, dogmatic, and a flagrant example of the way in which some disciplines exceed their rights and capacities. The question *whether* religion is a matter of revelation, as it claims to be, is precisely the one which requires vigorous and reverent exploration. Comparative religion, valuable as it is, may have no other effect than that of deepening the cynicism and relativism which are so common in the average student mind. If the teacher is himself an advanced and disciplined scholar, it is his duty to take a position to show that some religions are better than others and to show why. Religion can be very evil as well as very good, and it is one task of a university to help students to know this. Theology, therefore, should be normative and not merely descriptive.

Theology ought to be connected with practical experience whenever possible. There ought to be, in every university, something which bears the same relationship to theological teaching that the laboratory bears to scientific teaching. This is wonderfully possible in a university, providing the same people who do the teaching are charged with the task of fostering the practical religious life of the academic community. Just as research, experimentation, and teaching help each other, so the person who teaches the philosophy or history or literature of religion ought to put his ideas into practice by having a responsibility for the public worship of his university and the fostering of religious life in a thousand ways. The system at Harvard, in which the Dean of the Divinity School is also the Chairman of the Board of Preachers, seems to be in right ordering. Apart from such an arrangement the theologian may come to live a closeted and sterile life and may yield more easily to the temptation to present his courses devoid of religious feeling. We should think very poorly of the medical school in which the professors of medicine were men who never did practical medical work, and we ought to think equally poorly of a university in which the practical university life and the academic teaching of religion are essentially unconnected. We cannot expect to have any good theology in a university unless the university stresses worship as well as study. Discussion is not enough.

Our modern universities are great arenas of pagan culture, places of immense danger as well as hope for the future. Without the proper guidance they may turn out students who have technical ability, but little moral integrity and no worthwhile pattern of existence. Our young people need, in addition to a knowledge of the facts of history and of nature, a general philosophic structure in which they can put the details of their knowledge, and inspiration for courageous living in the midst of difficult times. There is no good reason why a scholar cannot seek to give these to his students and, at the same time, keep his academic integrity. He is likely to be a far better teacher if he is a deep believer, and he is likely to be more truly devout if he subjects all his conclusions to the most rigorous critical inquiry of which man's mind is capable. The purpose of theology in a university is to provide knowledge and, at the same time, to help in the promotion of something better than knowledge: a reasonable faith by which to live.

Reprinted from *Religion in Life,* Autumn Number, 1942.

8
The Minister's Study

However sure we may be that lay religion is both our hope and our ultimate ideal, there is no doubt that our best immediate chance of affecting the religious life of our country is through the ordinary parish ministry. Unless the average minister of the average church is a creative force, we are not really likely to see a new day of spiritual reconstruction in our time. Unless the voices most often heard are prophetic voices, the church tends to become just another human institution, not worse than others and very little better. Accordingly, what goes on in the minds and hearts of our thousands of clergymen is of very great importance, and any efforts we can make to improve the effectiveness of the average minister are efforts well spent.

My observation of the rank and file of American ministers, of whom I have the privilege of knowing a great many, is that they are mostly good men, but that they exhibit some glaring weaknesses that need not be. They are not, on the whole, as carefully trained as are doctors and lawyers, but nearly all of them are moved by a deep sense of vocation and can be counted on to perform their duties conscientiously. Very few of them are fundamentally self-seeking, and most of them are not lazy. Our hope lies in the fact that the major failures of the ministry are not intrinsic, but are failures which might reasonably be expected to yield to intelligent treatment and effort. The situation is often pathetic, but it is seldom hopeless, in view of the fact that most ministers seem conscious of need and are basically eager to perform their noble tasks as well as they can.

One of the truly shocking facts about our present-day ministry is the way in which so many ministers are living lives of personal frustration. The physicians of souls are lamentably unable to heal themselves. Much of the trouble lies in an almost constant conflict between the average minister's idealization of his own job and the actual life he leads. He feels in his heart that he ought to spend much time in meditation, in prayer, and in study, in order to bring creative insight to the needy people who are looking to him for help; but as the years go on, he finds that this side of his life becomes almost negligible. He feels he ought to be a prophet, but he knows very well that in fact he is a kind of business manager. His major energies are employed in conducting drives, planning promotional activities, answering letters, checking on printing, and general administration. The church becomes a kind of club, and the pastor is the manager of the club, looking after the details of organization. Some men rebel against this but do not know how to become free from it, while others, though they do some complaining, really welcome the chore-boy life they lead, because it protects them from that revealing encounter with the white sheet of paper lying on the study desk. They think they hate the telephone; but when the time for writing comes, they welcome the alibi which the steadily ringing telephone provides.

I know personally many ministers who actually use a study very little in any particular week. Most of them have what they *call* studies, but the real character of these rooms is that of offices. These rooms, whether in home or church, are places where the weekly calendar is prepared and some letters written, but they are not primarily scenes of struggle over big ideas. Seldom are they places where serious books are read, and still more seldom are they places where thoughts are laboriously put on paper. Many ministers must feel a twinge of conscience when they read in *Barchester Towers* the familiar description of Archdeacon Grantly in his study. The famous Trollope character wished to give the impression that his study was the scene of nothing but intellectual labor, but in fact he spent part of his time there, stretched on a couch, reading light novels.

Often a man will keep thinking all week that he will get some time to sit in his study, but day after day there are the funerals, weddings, luncheon clubs, golf games, dinners, and the counseling of needy human beings in such profusion and rapid succession that finally the best the man can do is to have a little while alone on Saturday night with Sunday morning already staring him in the face. Often he is conscious that he has not read a single book, that he has not even kept up his devotional reading, and that there has not been a single hour set aside for quiet meditation. In this predicament the frustrated man jots down an outline of a few platitudes, decides to adorn them with some selected anecdotes, and perhaps even selects a Bible text to go with them, the selection being made by use of the concordance.

The vocal ministry which comes in this way may seem vigorous and fresh for a time, but after a while the surface wears thin and the basic shoddiness of the procedure is evident to all thoughtful hearers. It is ministry of this kind that is in many localities failing to hold the attention of those who are among the most concerned people. We do our best to convince these people that they ought to share in the local Christian community, but often they are disgusted when they actually try it. It is this situation which we must change and change rapidly, or we shall fail. I cannot speak with any assurance about Roman Catholics, but I am very sure that, unless our Protestant efforts are soon placed on a much higher level, we shall cease to be a significant factor in our total culture, even though our organizations continue a vestigial existence.

Of all the problems which the minister faces, two stand out above others, the problem of pride and the problem of time. Pride is a problem because the minister is among the most complimented of men, and some men are foolish enough to take constant praise seriously, just as they are foolish enough to take constant criticism seriously. Since others have dealt with the problem of pride, my present emphasis is on the problem of time. We must learn a discipline of time in which we are hard with ourselves for the sake of the noble cause we serve. We must learn to distinguish between the merely good use of time and the very best use of time, and we must learn to live our daily lives in chapters. Counseling is a good thing; but if we counsel all day long, we shall come to the place where we have nothing really important to say to those who seek our spiritual help. Attendance at luncheons is good, but it is easy to attend so many that the books which would make us more effective lie at home with their leaves uncut. The wise minister will do many things, but he will do them at different times, and he will be especially concerned that the trivial will not so dominate the situation that no time is left for the more profound.

A major difficulty in this connection is that of tearing oneself away from what seem like human needs. Is it not a wicked thing to take the telephone off the hook when needy people might call? Is it not harsh and cruel to go to your attic to study when living men and women are seeking advice? Should we put meditation above service? Fortunately, in dealing with this question we have not only sound reason to aid us, but also the known example of Christ. We know that there were times when he left the multitudes and went apart, alone. He was not being disloyal to people by this removal, but rather more loyal, because he could come back refreshed. It also helps us in this problem if we face frankly the fact that many of the tasks which sap our energies and destroy study habits are not important at all. The members of countless churches use their pastors for trivial duties simply because they consider the pastors easily available and hired for such purposes. The members have a great responsibility in learning to know when *not* to telephone.

A minister's library is a pitiless revelation of his mind and of his usefulness. Spend two hours alone with his books and you know a great deal about a man. Which books are well worn? What types predominate? Are the books marked with his own comments in the margins, showing that he has read them thoughtfully and creatively? Some ministers lean largely to books of sermons, and these are nearly always second- or third-rate men! One of the really terrible things about this situation is that such men actually preach other men's sermons, and sometimes they do so without giving credit. No doubt they argue that a good sermon is worth using more than once and that the *people* don't care who wrote it first. It may be that people do not care, and many of them may never know the difference; but such dishonest action does something damaging to the preacher himself. The habit of leaning on others grows, and the undisciplined life through the week doesn't seem so bad since there is always another of Dr. Fosdick's sermons on the shelf waiting to be used at the last minute.

The worst mistake about using other men's sermons is that the ideas, however excellent they may be, lack reality. It is hard for a man to use words with conviction and power when he has not thought of them in the turmoil of his own brain. Some men do better than others at this, but I could not possibly read a printed sermon, even the best, and make it sound at all convincing. It is seldom that I can make an old address of my own sound convincing. It seems so cold and lifeless to me that I cannot really believe what I am saying. The result is that, though naturally I use some of the same general ideas more than once, I am forced by my own desire for vigorous presentation to put these ideas in new contexts and prepare them again. It may be the same old metal, but it must be newly minted each time if it is to become intellectual legal tender.

Even more damaging than the book of sermons is the book of anecdotes. If all of them could be burned, we might experience a great advance in the prophetic ministry. Stories undoubtedly have a place in the effective presentation of ideas, the practice of Christ being sufficient to make this clear; but there is a world of difference between stories we meet in common life or general reading and

those which are deliberately sought out as an adornment. There
is a story in the experience of Timothy Dwight which I often tell
and which seems to me effective, but I am sure that it would make
me gag if I had gleaned it from a book of "sermon illustrations."
I got the story as one unexpected by-product of the laborious
reading of a long biography of the famous Yale president, and
after that it partly belonged to me. One of the worst things about
the stories secured from collections is that the sensitive hearer
recognizes them right away. The hearer can almost see the preacher on Saturday night, needing desperately an illustration, looking
in the section on "Work" or "Loyalty" or "Peace." Men who
cannot find good preaching material without such devices might
be better occupied in some other vocation.

The book of stock poems is almost as bad as the book of anecdotes, and again the trouble is that a man gets something without
earning it. It is one thing to get a great idea for a sermon by
reading Matthew Arnold and stumbling excitedly on "The Buried
Life," but it is quite another to crib the idea by looking in a poetic
anthology under "Love." It is one thing to read the book of Job
and be stabbed awake by the words "To cause it to rain on the
earth, where no man is," so that we plan a sermon on the foolishness of supposing that man is the measure of all things, but it is
quite another to find this pregnant text in a collection of "sermon
thoughts." Nearly all the best preaching comes from ideas that are
earned the hard way. The nuggets mean more if we find them
ourselves.

The reading that we ought to be doing in our studies is, for the
most part, reading that is not undertaken with immediate sermon-
ic or homiletic needs in mind, just as the best farming is done by
men who are constantly building the soil and not merely fertilizing
for the immediate crop. If a man is always reading important
books such as major biographies, essays, literary studies, science,
philosophy, and theology, he can hardly fail to have a significant
message. In such reading we run into exciting ideas in the most

unexpected places. Frequently the material is not something which we can lift bodily to our own addresses, but rather something which stimulates our own thought. Sometimes the thought produced is very different from that which produces it, but we could not arrive at it without this outside aid. When the idea came to me that ours is a cut-flower civilization, the idea had a certain originality in my own mind, but it was stimulated by another idea in a certain book. Only one man, Charles Clayton Morrison, has ever guessed what book that was. The author of the book would hardly believe it, however, when I told him.

Far too much of our reading is of the digested and over-easy type. I have no antipathy to the *Reader's Digest,* except that it takes up the time of men who ought to do their own digesting, but the popularity of this magazine is very revealing. If we consume only predigested material, some of our organs deteriorate. The average minister certainly uses too much of his precious reading time on newspapers and magazines and too little time on books. I am glad to have known one or two prophetic minds who were wise enough to postpone the reading of the newspaper until the creative work of the day was done. It is not a ridiculous discipline for a concerned minister to refuse to take a morning paper. There is no great loss in this practice because, if some world-shaking event occurs, the word will get out in plenty of time.

Much of a minister's serious reading should be in fields other than those usually termed religious because real religion is coterminous with common life. A thoughtful man soon discovers the devotional paradox to the effect that the deepest inspiration frequently arises from secular literature, while that literature which is intentionally inspiring so often palls. The great novels of the past deserve a rereading and may bring us insight when we little expect it.

All the best reading is done with a pen in hand. The advantage is that the reader is himself active and doing something about the ideas. Little help comes to the passive observer or to the passive reader. We should underline striking sentences, query doubtful passages, and make our own index in the back of the book, so that later we can find significant sections with speed and ease. I have long been grateful to the man who started me on this practice twenty-five years ago.

It is a natural step from reading with a pen to using a pen without the book. More and more, as a minister advances in maturity, he should write rather than read. Whether he writes for publication or not is not of paramount importance. The important thing is that a man should discipline his mind by putting his ideas down in the clearest way possible to him. The ideas may not be grand, but they are at least his own; and the very effort to state them makes a mind grow. I hold that a man is not likely to rise to the fullness of his powers as a minister unless he writes something serious every week of the world. This may be a sermon, it may be an essay, and it may be a long insertion in a man's own notebook, but there is not much likelihood of growth without something of the kind. What I should like to find would be a group of ministers representing many ages and many denominations but united by one hard discipline, the discipline of writing. The minimum demand would be that each member of this disciplined society would undertake to spend four consecutive hours in every week writing. This would have to be a period with no telephone calls, no magazine reading, no conferences, and no callers. To meet these conditions it would be necessary for many men to get entirely away from their families and other responsibilities.

The indispensable tool of every minister is a notebook. Naturally a man carries this with him at all times and must be ready to put ideas into it as they come. Sometimes we proceed on the erroneous assumption that we can remember ideas without jotting them down, but we are almost always wrong in this judgment. The greatest advantage of writing ideas down is that the very writing stimulates other ideas, and before long these begin to form in clusters. Soon a notebook is full of such clusters at various stages of development. A man with such a notebook is never in the quandary of wondering what there is about which he can preach. He will have such a wealth of ideas that his problem will always be the problem of selection.

One final word concerns the handling of material for future use. Each man must work out some system of filing because the material is abundant. There are old notes, manuscripts, clippings, and an endless variety of pamphlets. Probably there is no perfect way of keeping these materials in order, but the experience of most men indicates that a system of open folders is best. These are better than envelopes because materials can be added and subtracted with maximum ease. If a man cannot afford to buy a filing cabinet, open orange boxes serve the purpose admirably and usually cost nothing. The major point to make about a file is that of going over it frequently. A wise student will frequently thumb through the files of notes, and he will usually find that some unexpected idea will arise. It is these ideas that are precious, and the purpose of study is the facilitation of their growth in both numbers and power.

It is a good thing for ministers to serve the public and be friendly and all, but we shall never see the recovery we desire until the friendly men who serve our churches are also studious men. In this direction lies our next line of advance.

Reprinted from *The Ministry*, edited by J. Richard Spann, Abingdon-Cokesbury Press, 1949.

9
The Love
of the Difficult

The greatest of all sciences is the science of decision. Nothing can take its place. There are many sciences that can collect the facts, but these are essentially elementary. Finally a decision has to be made, like the choice that President Kennedy made, in 1962, about the presence of Russian missile bases in Cuba. There were the facts; there were the photographs; there were the reports; but the decision was something else, and decision in any important matter is always hard because there are always alternatives. And the top man never gets the easy one.

We would love in our country, if we could, to have machines that would do the work of choice. We have been overimpressed with the computers. There are people who really seem to believe that if you have a big enough computing machine, decision would be taken care of. This is nonsense. This is not possible; it will not be possible because it would be inconsistent with the entire human predicament. The machine may analyze the data, and this is really not very hard. A computer is an adding machine vastly amplified and made more complex. But its answers are already there, as they are in elementary logic. If you know that all A's are B's and all B's are C's, the conclusion of the syllogism requires no judgment, for you can test it on a machine. Here is no leap; here is no break; here is no responsibility; and therefore it can be made mechanical. But the important things in this world cannot be made mechanical.

Whenever we find something that is really making a difference, there is a person involved. The fundamental factor is neither the program nor the building, but always the human factor. The best school is the school with the best teachers. It is that simple. This is why the great Charles Malik has given us his brilliant aphorism, "Find the good teacher and forget everything else." You may think that is an overstatement. Perhaps it is, but it sometimes takes overstatement to make things clear.

If this is at all true, then the decisions that headmasters are making about their teachers are very hard ones because the quality of these teachers will determine, in the long run, what goes on in the school. Somebody has to decide. You cannot put this on a slide rule, now or ever. Decision is hard because the answers are indeterminate and because it is the glory of man to be indeterminate. The only way to have the science of decision work is to build such a people and such an atmosphere that you have reason to hope that the decisions will be made somewhere near right. That is absolutely all that you can do.

This is the essence of our lives: we are vulnerable. We shall always be vulnerable. We shall never know how to make choices perfectly. Yet we must make them, for the failure to make a decision is itself a decision. If you say that you will not decide whether to let the weeds go to seed in your garden, you have already decided; life moves on. What we want to do more than anything else, for those under our care, is to make something like a science of decision possible, and it will be different from every other science in the world.

I want to emphasize that in developing this science, the love of the difficult is paramount. This phrase is taken from the *Letters* of the famous German poet Rainer Maria Rilke. If you have read the *Letters* you could not have missed the page in which he said, "The one thing that I most want to say to the young man is, 'Learn to love the difficult.' " He went on to say that if you have learned to love the difficult, life will not necessarily be easy, but you will be over a great divide. Nothing of any importance is easy. It is not easy to learn logarithms; it is not easy to learn grammar.

If we mean to accomplish anything of any significance, we must tell the young people that life is difficult. If one heresy can be said to be worse than another, it is this notion that we must always make the little dears happy. This approach is damaging. It is softening to any society, and the independent schools are fortunately in a position to turn their backs upon it completely.

At the beginning of the Fourth Book of the *Republic* one of Socrates' questioners asks whether the guardians will be happy. The reason this question is asked is that the road laid out for them is very hard, without material rewards, and with a big dose of mathematics and of what we call science. Socrates answers in an unforgettable way: "Our aim in founding the State was not the disproportionate happiness of any one class." The relevant question is: Will they be excellent? Will they find their true vocation? Will they have responsibility? Will they live up to the responsibility? Will they help to produce a better social order?

Aristotle developed the great doctrine that the only way to get happiness is to forget it. Every one of us knows the hedonistic paradox that the most unhappy people in the world are the people who are trying to be happy.

There will be no love of the difficult without a frank acceptance of discipline in our lives. Everyone can recognize that the undisciplined life is practically worthless. A human life that goes in the path of least resistance will give no more usable power than will the stream that flows all over the bottom land. The only way to make a stream produce power is to put it between sharp high banks, run it through a man-made gorge where it is controlled, and, because it is controlled, the implicit power is available.

You cannot learn any science without an immense discipline. Think how long it takes to learn to use a microscope or a telescope. During my days at Stanford, when I was invited by the head of the observatory on Mount Wilson to look through the telescope, I saw the difference between him and me. He said that he had trained the telescope on vast nebulae a million light years away. I saw nothing. I believed him, but I could not verify the existence of the nebulae in my own experience. He had disciplined his eyes over thirty years to see what could be seen through that telescope, and I had not. This was the difference.

The same is true in music, in athletics, in every phase of life where any kind of excellence is required. People say, "Oh, yes, but remember the discipline has to be voluntary." There is a sense in which that is true and a sense in which that is false. It has to be voluntary in the sense that only the person can put the pressure on his own life. But if you wait for most young people to start their own voluntary discipline, you will wait a long time. Most young people will not themselves initiate their discipline. Though you and I cannot enforce it, we can encourage it. We can encourage it by making a standard and by adhering to it. I am talking about the firmness by which the student knows that the teacher means business.

One of the chief ways to encourage the self-discipline of the student is for the teacher himself to demonstrate discipline. He can do it by having his courses well and carefully organized. A teacher must use every available minute at the beginning of an hour as though it were the last hour on earth. The mood becomes infectious: by starting and stopping on time, by knowing what the assignment is and expecting it to come in and by not being unduly patient about the poor little papers that are written at the last possible minute, using only a margin of the abilities which the students have. The teacher needs to show by his own example the joy that comes in a full extension of our powers. It is great to lift, on occasion, every ounce that you can lift. It is great sometimes to write so hard that you cannot possibly produce another sentence. It is great to run, sometimes, as fast as you can run. The student knows well whether the teacher is doing this himself. You cannot be a missionary for anything which you do not have in your own life. We need to be more demanding, especially with ourselves. We have much greater powers than we have ever demonstrated.

Here is a parable. When many of us were in college, we were told that it was impossible for a human being to run a mile in less than four minutes. I remember hearing it said that it would never be done. Then a medical student in England did it. But that is not the most surprising fact about the story. The most surprising fact is that, during the next few years, it was done thirty-seven times, and last summer, at Palo Alto, it was done by four men in one race. How do you account for that? There was no rapid change in the track. There was no sudden transformation in the physique or in the feeding. The only way to account for it is expectancy. Thirty-seven other men came to realize that it could be done.

Every teacher knows he is faced every day with young people who are employing only a tiny margin of their powers. Here is where we can bring to bear our religious motive. For a man to be less than he might be is itself a blasphemy. We are made in God's image. *We are made to make,* to produce. The creation of man is a very serious business, and for us to take this image of God in our own lives and deface it and fail to bring it to fulfillment is not merely bad scholarship or bad citizenship; it is bad religion. God made man responsible, and we are our brothers' keepers. This is why we are teaching. The teacher with a strong religious motivation has a tremendous reason to try to develop each person, especially if he sees him as one for whom Christ died, who is, for that reason, of infinite value. He is bound to look upon each one with a sense of urgency. The greatest of all tragedies is the tragedy of waste. To have something fail to flower, when it could have done so, is a sin, for which all involved are responsible. If you go to your schools and make the love of the difficult your motive, this is not something separate from your faith; this is something intrinsic to your faith.

Have you come to the place in your association where you are quite frank and unapologetic about your faith in the teaching of the young? I know there was a time when the popular fad was never to make a witness, never to take a stand. We sometimes have students like that. A recent convocation speaker said, "I simply want to say unequivocally that I am trying to be a servant of Jesus Christ and one who unworthily is in his kingdom." A few students were up in arms. What does that matter? If we cannot be a Christian college and let that kind of thing be said, we had better be out of business.

I hope that you will have the urge in this love of the difficult to give a witness to an unapologetic faith, providing you have such a faith. Never let anybody say that you are thereby putting yourself forward. You are not. You are not bragging about your own character. In fact, the more you have such a faith, the more you know how unworthy your character is. You are not telling who you are. You are telling *whose* you are. Nothing of any importance in the science of decision comes by detachment. We do not get close to God by a lecture on God. We do not get close to the church by a lecture on the church. You never understand it unless you are in it. Only the involved can know.

Reprinted from *Education for Decision,* Seabury Press, 1963.

10
Acropolis and Areopagus

Two hundred one years ago Dr. Samuel Johnson, in his famous tour of the Hebrides, stood among the ruins of Iona and uttered the following memorable words: "Far from me and from my friends, be such frigid philosophy as may conduct us indifferent and unmoved over any ground which has been dignified by wisdom, bravery or virtue. That man is little to be envied whose patriotism would not gain force upon the plain of Marathon, or whose piety would not grow warmer among the ruins of Iona." Now you and I are among other ruins, those of the temples of the Athenian Acropolis, and not far from the bare top of the Areopagus. As Dr. Johnson was moved in the famous scene of Scotland, so, if we are sensitive, we may be moved as we visit the scenes connected with the glorious history of ancient Greece. Once you are on the Acropolis, there is no farther that you can go!

The shell of the building behind you may reasonably be called the most beautiful building of the world, even in spite of its ruined state. Though only the walls and most of the columns remain, this structure is appealing, chiefly because of the delicacy of the proportions. Long ago, in 1687, when the Turks were using the temple as a powder magazine, a Venetian shell caused the explosion which blew off the roof and destroyed most of the interior. Much later Lord Elgin (1766-1841) arranged for the transfer to London of many of the carved decorations, particularly the Metopes. Now, for 150 years these beautiful carvings have been housed in the British Museum, where they are known as the "Elgin Marbles" and have become a major tourist attraction.

In some ways it seems a shame that they were taken from here

73

to London. In another way, it is a blessing because in London they have not deteriorated. If they had remained in the open air, there would have been serious erosion. As it is, further erosion has been avoided, and the marbles are safe from being stolen.

Part of the amazement of visitors here comes as they see how beautiful the Doric style of construction is, even without its decorations. The proportions of this famous building, which please the eye so much, are nine to four. In order to verify this, you may have noticed that I walked around the entire structure, just prior to this lecture, carefully counting my steps. As I walked I thought again of the brilliant planners who made the crucial decisions more than 2,400 years ago. The more we contemplate their work, particularly that of Phidias, supervisor of the entire work, the more we are filled with wonder. There are many subtle things about this building which we miss at first. For example, the line of the base appears to be absolutely horizontal, but this is not the case. It actually arches slightly because the ancient architects were such good psychologists that they knew that, if the line were actually straight, it would look to our eyes as though it sagged in the middle. Amazingly, the builders knew exactly how much to lift the flat arch to make it satisfying to the eyes of the beholder.

We are keenly aware, as we gather here, of the flowering of the human spirit which occurred in this city in the fifth century before Christ. What occurred was simultaneous brilliant development in a variety of fields, including philosophy, architecture, historical writing, and drama. Many of the cultural standards of subsequent centuries were established here, with a combination of excellence rare anywhere in the world. Here Socrates was born in 469; here Pericles died in 429, after his brilliant political leadership of the government; here Herodotus originated the writing of history as we understand it; here lived Thucydides and Xenophon, who continued the work Herodotus had started; here were produced the plays of Aeschylus, Euripides, and Sophocles; and, above all, here Plato established his Academy and wrote his immortal dialogues. How could one small city-state produce so much? How could there be such a galaxy of brilliant persons?

We shall never know completely the answer to this question, but we do know part of it. The burst of new life came, in large measure, from a sense of gratitude! The Greeks, and especially the Athenians, were convinced that they had been saved miraculously from the domination of the Persian power, which would have ended their freedom. The Greeks experienced two Persian invasions, the first at Marathon in 490 BC and the second in 480, the latter involving the destruction of much of the city of Athens. All of subsequent history would have been vastly different if either of these invasions, in both of which the Greeks were outnumbered, had been successful. That is why Dr. Johnson's patriotism gained force as he thought of the plain of Marathon, twenty-six miles from where we are now gathered.

Because of tremendous gratitude, the Athenians decided to rebuild their city with real grandeur. We must never forget that the main structures on the Acropolis are expressions of a mood of thanksgiving, on the part of people who believed that they had experienced a divine deliverance from slavery. Because the Persian king had decreed that the men of Athens were to be brought to him as slaves, the soldiers at Marathon knew how high the price of failure would be.

The blooming of Athens was reasonably late. We understand this better when we realize that the major events here came a full one hundred years after the crucial steps in the lives of both Confucius and Buddha. The enlightenment of Buddha under the Bo-tree came in the year 528 BC and Confucius started his school in China in that same year, but it was not until almost a century later that the structures here were completed and the flowering of Athens came into being. Our debt to Pericles is great indeed, for it was his ambition, not only to beautify the scene, but also to bring in philosophers, in order to make Athens a notable center of learning. Before Pericles, this area then was really the west, the centers of civilization being much farther east. In truth, Athens was the frontier!

The Battle of Thermopylae came ten years after the Battle of Marathon, in the year 480 BC. At that time a great horde of Persians came across from where Istanbul now is, mostly by land, following in reverse the same order that we shall take when we leave Philippi to go to Turkey in a few days. The invasion in 480 was directed by Xerxes, who expected to overwhelm by sheer numbers. The Spartan king, Leonidas, led his soldiers north to meet the Persians, making their stand at Thermopylae, which was then a narrow pass through which the invaders had to come. Next week, as we travel, we shall see the location of the pass and shall be reminded of the inscription, "Tell the Lacedemonians that we died here, in obedience to their laws."

The Spartans, for all their bravery, did not stop the Persian invasion at Thermopylae. All of the three hundred who tried to hold the pass were killed, and the Persian force moved on south, even to where we now are. The city of Athens was sacked and the earlier structures on the Acropolis were utterly destroyed. But that was not the end of the story! The final defeat of the Persians came, not by land, but on the water, as the Battle of Salamis was fought in the Saronic Gulf to the west of Athens, Salamis being the base for the Athenian fleet. The battle, which occurred September 28, 480 BC, was decisive in that the Persian navy retreated after the conflict, and never came again.

The virtual destruction of Athens by Xerxes was something of a blessing because it permitted a fresh start. The decision to rebuild the Temple of Athens came twenty-three years after the departure of Xerxes in 457 BC. The actual building was begun in 447. Though the dedication occurred nineteen years later, in 438, the work of decoration was still going on as late as 433. In short, all of the work was accomplished in the lifetime of Socrates, who actually seems to have been one of the stonecutters.

The building of the Parthenon was a stupendous undertaking,

with hundreds of separate tasks, as individual workmen contracted for the fluting of the columns and all the carving. What you
might not realize, looking at it today, is that this was very highly
decorated 2,400 years ago. When Socrates and his students looked
up here they saw a painted exterior with exceedingly bright colors.
Though the painting of marble is a surprising idea to modern
people, there is no doubt that the Greeks performed it. The idea
was to make the structure as stunning and bright and attractive
as it could be. Of course, with the years, all of that has now
disappeared.

The Agora, or Marketplace of ancient Athens, on the level area
below us, was the scene of the major teaching career of Socrates.
You can see this very clearly as you climb to the top of Mars' Hill.
As the young men of Athens gathered around Socrates, the intellectual encounter proceeded almost wholly by dialogue. One of
these young men was Plato, who was only twenty-eight years old
when his beloved mentor was executed by the democracy. One of
the major steps in intellectual history occurred when, in the fourth
century BC, Plato decided to keep the ideas of his teacher alive
by writing the Socratic dialogues. For these we are supremely
grateful because, through them, the ideas which once were limited
to a select few have become the prized possession of millions, in
distant countries of which the Socratics could not even dream.

The guides have told you that the small hill, overlooking the
Agora, is called Mars' Hill, or, in Greek, the Areopagus, the two
words having the same denotation. It was there, about AD 50,
when the Parthenon was already more than four hundred years
old, that the first Christian group arrived. The juxtaposition of
these two hills is a symbol of the conjunction of the Hellenic
thought and the Christian faith. Nearly two thousand years ago,
the Greek religions withered and died, just as a new faith based
on the living Christ began to emerge. The philosophy of Greece,
however, continued and became very important in western culture, continuing, in great measure, as part of the intellectual struc-

ture of the new faith that Paul and his companions introduced when they visited Mars' Hill. As one faith was dying, another was coming to birth.

The book of Acts tells how the apostle Paul and a few companions had an encounter with some of the local intellectuals. The Areopagus was then the scene of a building, housing what we should call the high court. Since the building disappeared long ago, there is nothing to see now except the bare top of the hill. The apostle Paul, standing in the middle of the Areopagus, said, "Men of Athens, I perceive that in every way you are very religious" (Acts 17:22, RSV). It is obvious that he looked up here and saw these gorgeous buildings which were really shrines. As he looked down into the Agora, there also he could see shrines. We know about them because the American School of Classical Studies has removed about six feet of silt and thereby revealed the foundations of buildings, some of which had religious significance. Thus Paul continued, "As I passed along, and observed the objects of your worship, I found also an altar with this inscription 'To an unknown god.' What therefore you worship as unknown, this I proclaim to you. The God who made the world and everything in it, being Lord of heaven and earth, does not live in shrines made by man" (Acts 17:23-24, RSV).

The courage which it took to make such an utterance is almost overwhelming because the shrines were honored and some of them were truly magnificent, but Paul understood that there was something better than shrines. The message delivered on the Areopagus has its own nobility, as the architecture of the temples has its nobility. As a teacher of philosophy, it has been my dream for forty-five years that I might some day pay my respects to both kinds of nobility by lecturing to students in Athens. I have now done so.

(A lecture delivered at Athens, Greece, April 19, 1974, as part of an educational tour called "Adventure in Living.")

11
The Self
and the Community

The most important fact that we know about the universe is that it has persons in it. Each finite person is an occasion for hope—and also a potential danger because it is of the very nature of the personal reality that it should be unstable and even liable to self-destruction. The rock cannot destroy itself by a false conception of its meaning, but persons can do this and have, in fact, done so in many instances. The recent visits of men to the moon have made more vivid what we already knew about the amazing stability of rocks. The sample stones brought back to earth by the men of Apollo 15 appear not to have changed at all during the thousands of years when the life of persons has been changing all of the time. It is because persons are beings who are engaged in the emergence of novelty that perfect historical prediction is impossible.

We often hear the complaint that we do much worse in human development than we do in scientific development and that an equal expenditure of money would alter the disparity, but the complaint is fundamentally naive. Of course it is harder to manage persons than it is to manage atoms because atoms have no freedom and therefore no sin. The management of human life is not only difficult and disappointing, but also exhilarating; and it will always be so because of the kind of reality with which we are dealing. Much of the instability of human organization arises from the relationship between the self and the community, the emphasis upon both of these being necessary for the authentic development of personhood. Civilizations are essentially unstable formations because they are created and sustained by beings who are always oscillating between two poles.

My own interest in the question of the right ordering of the claims of personal identity and social responsibility was much enhanced by the West Lectures delivered by Reinhold Niebuhr at Stanford University early in 1944. I had the good fortune to be Professor Niebuhr's host and to be able to rejoice in the splendid reception accorded the lectures, which were later published with the title *The Children of Light and the Children of Darkness.* The book, which may be rightly regarded as the most brilliant work of a brilliant Christian thinker, was given the subtitle *A Vindication of Democracy and a Critique of Its Traditional Defense.* Since the death of Professor Niebuhr, I am glad to envisage my essay as a slight recognition of personal indebtedness to him. The subject of this essay was one very familiar to Niebuhr, his second and crucial lecture in the series being entitled "The Individual and the Community."

Central to Reinhold Niebuhr's analysis was the recognition of the inadequacy of the familiar secular defenses of democratic theory, especially those which stem from the doctrine of Rousseau. I suppose it was Niebuhr who first made me see that the Christian thinkers have, on the whole, been far more sophisticated in their handling of the problems of democracy than have the pure secularists. Having, as their support, the doctrine of original sin, Christian thinkers have often been able to avoid the twin dangers of according too much power to the isolated individual and too much power to the collective. Above all, the ideal of self-sufficiency can easily be recognized, in Christian philosophy, as both untrue and politically dangerous. "The ideal of self-sufficiency, so exalted in our liberal culture," said Niebuhr, "is recognized in Christian thought as one form of the primal sin. For self-love, which is the root of all sin, takes two social forms. One of them is the domination of other life by the self. The second is the sin of isolationism" (*The Children of Light,* p. 55).

The crucial mistake is concentrating on one set of perils while neglecting the opposite ones. In short, the true way is narrow and there are wide gutters on both sides. It is no gain if, in a determined effort to stay out of one gutter, a person falls into the opposite one. Error comes by failure to recognize that danger is multiple. This seems to be the practical significance of Christ's warning about the double danger in the words, "Beware of the leaven of the Pharisees, and of the leaven of Herod" (Mark 8:15). Reinhold Niebuhr caught our attention when he said, "Preoccupation with the perils of collective forms of ambition produces social theories which emphasize freedom at the expense of order, ending finally in the philosophy of anarchism. Preoccupation with the perils of individual inordinateness, on the other hand, allows the fear of anarchy to bear the fruit of connivance with tyranny" (*The Children of Light,* p. 47).

It is obvious, when we think about it, that total concentration on either the self or the community is destructive of human values. The cult of individualism, if consistently applied, would make any genuine civilization impossible. This is because the really separated individual would not be able either to learn from others or to pass on to others any accumulated wisdom about life. We can see something of the potential danger in the recently popular and thoroughly vulgar admonition, "Do your own thing." Taken seriously, this admonition would make persons into separated monads uninfluenced by one another. There would be no value in history and no possibility of group creation of the future. Indeed, all concern for the welfare of others would be undermined. Freedom is an undoubted value, but unless there is some limitation upon it, all other values are destroyed. Absolute freedom would mean absolute chaos.

The whole idea of the totally separated individual, following rules of his own making, is an idea which could not possibly be given embodiment. In any case, such an individual would not be a person and would represent an inner contradiction, for the wholly separated being is not even a self. Those who advocate uninhibited self-expression are really proposing an impossible dream. The completely separate self is a contradiction in terms, for if there is no consciousness of others, there is no self-consciousness. Important as the conception of personal identity may be, it cannot stand alone.

At the same time, the merely collective person is an intrinsic impossibility. Ants, as we all know, can do marvelous things, and they do them by collective efficiency. In Uganda I once saw an ant hill that was actually fourteen feet high. No ant, working alone, could possibly produce anything of this kind, but ants can do it as a community. It is important to recognize, however, that they pay a high price for their collective efficiency; they do not become persons at all! That development in this direction is a real danger for humans is shown by some features of life in modern China. History might, conceivably, move in this direction, but the consequent tragedy would be immense.

We are making a start on the philosophy of civilization when we realize that both individualism and collectivism represent flights from reality, for the real is neither the separated nor the undifferentiated. Just as the mere individual is an abstraction, so the mere community has no counterpart in reality. Society means nothing unless it is composed of individuals, each possessing his own dignity and enjoying his own rights. The way of wisdom, therefore, is to hold both conceptions in dynamic tension. Whenever we relieve the tension, settling simplistically for one or the other, we are already lost.

When we see the faddish swings of the pendulum in contemporary experience, we realize that the problem of the self and the community is by no means a merely academic one. Both extremes are observed every day, some persons being so confused that they actually demonstrate both errors in their own behavior. It is not uncommon, for instance, to encounter persons who, on one side, loudly affirm their right to express their individuality with no limitations, while, on the other side, they exhibit a servile conformity in dress, speech, choice of music, and general manner of life. The fact that the contradiction is not recognized to be such is part of the disease. It is a revelation of the triumph of irrationality.

A recognition of both the danger and the disease helps us to appreciate the role of the Christian intellectual. It is part of the task of Christians in the modern world to give real leadership, especially in the overcoming of confusion. The problem of modern man, in his oscillation between the two poles of self and community, is by no means a new one for the thoughtful Christian. Long ago a sophisticated answer was worked out, and it is a highly satisfactory one. It is the duty of thoughtful Christians not merely to tend their own spiritual gardens, but to share their insights and thus give assistance to mankind in general. Our responsibility is not primarily to the minority who are committed Christians, but to the vast majority of those who have no such commitment. This is part of what is meant by the penetration of the world which is represented by the metaphor of leaven. It is not sufficient for us to operate as a remnant, separated from the world. If there is something which is revealed, it is our duty to spread it as widely as possible. Our conviction is that the problem of the self and the community is one in regard to which some genuine light is available.

Always the great Christian word is *and*. In a number of situations the Christian insight is that *either-or* produces a heresy, while *and* can bring us close to reality. Examples of this in the Gospels are numerous. The great Commandment, as we all know, is a double one, involving not only the insight of Deuteronomy 6:5 but also that expressed in Leviticus 19:18. The originality lies in the conjunction of what must not be separated and in the consequent emergence of the paradox of double priority. The love of God is not real without the love of the brethren, and the love of the brethren is not real without the love of God. A similar use of the "holy conjunction" is that regarding the new and the old

(Matt. 13:52). That this wisdom is greatly needed in our contemporary culture is indicated by the way in which the masses swing mindlessly between the conformities of conservatism and the conformities of modernism. It is Christ's clear teaching that both new and old are required and that they are required together. Much foolishness about the claims of piety and the claims of social action could be overcome if the wisdom involved in the use of the holy conjunction were understood and followed.

The more we delve into the Scriptures, the more we understand the conjunctive genius of the Christian faith. One facet which is quickly illuminated is that of prayer. There is obviously a time when a person ought to pray alone, and this he will do if he follows Christ's own example, for we know that he went alone into a solitary place. But we also know that he prayed with others and even asserted that it was in the fellowship that his presence would be available. To settle for mere aloneness or mere togetherness is to miss the magnitude for which Christ calls. Another use of conjunction in prayer is represented by the equal emphasis upon spirituality and intelligence. The apostle Paul brings his remarkable good sense to bear on the issue by saying, "I will pray as I am inspired to pray, but I will also pray intelligently" (1 Cor. 14:15, NEB).

Beginning with the glory of *and* which is intrinsic to the gospel, Christian experience through the centuries has refined the conception, which is now applicable not merely to Christians but to all persons, that the self needs the community and that the community needs the self. On the one hand, there is abundant emphasis upon what is valid in individuality. The validity lies not in the fatuous belief that the individual is ever self-sufficient, but in the fact that the individual is always important. Each one is one and each is precious because each is the object of the divine concern. The notion that each person, regardless of race or sex or age or learning, is intrinsically valuable is one of the most revolutionary ideas in the world. When fully appreciated, it is bound to undermine all unfair discrimination and inequality of opportunity. This conception is not tied to the clearly erroneous belief that all people are equal in intelligence or in ability. If it were, it would be doomed at the start because factual inequality is part of the obvious truth about human life. In one sense, it is the foundation stone in Plato's social edifice and has been understood widely by his thoughtful successors in subsequent generations.

The Christian idea of all persons being "created" equal, which found its way into the American Declaration of Independence, is the profound idea that each individual is equally precious in God's eyes. Each, in spite of differences and in spite of factual inequality of powers, is made in God's image. Not a sparrow falls without the Father's affectionate concern, yet persons are far more precious than sparrows. It is no wonder, then, that the Divine Shepherd goes out to seek the *one* that is lost. In short, as Christians see reality, persons are not merely items in a mass called humanity, but each is single as an object of affection. The love of humanity is always an abstraction and sometimes an affectation, since the only adequate object of affection is the individual person.

Herein lies the rational appeal of the familiar doctrine of the dignity of the individual, which is always a derivative doctrine. It does not mean, of course, that persons are ultimately separate, but it does mean that persons are ultimately valuable. Therefore, we must ask of every proposal for social progress, "What will it do to persons?" In dealing with the race problem we must ask how individual dignity can be enhanced and maintained. The most terrible thing about human slavery while it lasted was that for great numbers of human beings it destroyed any possibility of individual dignity.

While the Christian understanding of personal reality has stressed the individual, it has also stressed equally the community. Herein lies one of the most striking contrasts between Christianity and several of the other religions which have emerged in world history. From the beginning, it was recognized that it is not possi-

ble to be a Christian alone, for it is only in the fellowship that the
new life can be known. So well was this understood in primitive
Christianity that the redemptive fellowship arose even before the
New Testament was produced. In fact, much of the New Testament was produced because of the felt needs of the existing fellow-
ships. Community was not something which was added to the
Christian revelation, but was something intrinsic to it. That is part
of what is involved in the affirmation, "Something greater than the
temple is here" (Matt. 12:6, RSV). A great deal of what went on
at the Temple in Jerusalem, like that which transpired at the
Parthenon, was individual religion.

In so far as we realize that it is impossible to be a Christian
alone, we recognize the necessity of the church, for the church is
simply the Christian community. How easily this point may be
missed we can see by reference to one of the greatest of twentieth-
century philosophers, Alfred North Whitehead. I owe much to
this good man, with whom I had a warm personal relationship.
He was both humble and kind, demonstrating in his own life many
of the specific Christian virtues. I can never forget how I sat and
listened to his now famous Lowell Lectures which, when they
were published in 1926, were entitled *Religion in the Making*. I
was impressed, of course, as a very young man, with his practical
conception of the role of philosophy. "If my view of the function
of philosophy is correct," he wrote in his preface to the first set
of Lowell Lectures, "it is the most effective of all the intellectual
pursuits. It builds cathedrals before the workmen have moved a
stone, and it destroys them before the elements have worn down
their arches." This is heady stuff, and, young as I was, I knew that
I was fortunate in being able to sit at the feet of a genuine sage.

What is most surprising about Whitehead's one specifically
religious book is that its most quoted sentence is clearly wrong.
Religion, the great man said, is what a man does with his solitari-
ness. This is an excellent illustration of the conception that error
is truth in isolation. Whitehead's mistake lay not in emphasizing

one pole, but in emphasizing it without equal reference to the other pole. Whatever religion Whitehead was referring to in his famous definition, he was certainly not referring to Christianity, for the definition would eliminate the church, and Christianity without the church would be something utterly foreign to what we have experienced.

Christian thinkers have recognized all along that their proposed solution of the problem of the self and the community involves genuine paradox. At first view, self-sufficiency and responsibility to others seem to be incompatible. Even the child in Sunday School feels something of the tension which is involved in two texts which appear close together in the New Testament. How can we reconcile "Bear one another's burdens" (Gal. 6:2) and "Each man will have to bear his own load" (Gal. 6:5)? This is, indeed, a paradox, but it is part of the sophistication of Christian thinking that paradox is necessary to the expression of whatever is profound. We dare not refer to the greatness of man unless we refer, equally and contemporaneously, to the littleness of man. Herein lies the immense appeal of the famous opening lines of *A Tale of Two Cities.* Dickens avoided being simplistic about the period of the French Revolution by beginning: "It was the best of times, it was the worst of times."

There is a deep sense in which each man must carry his own load, for no other person fully understands what the load is. We shall never have a good society if people expect to be pensioners of a welfare state with all services being rendered for them; but, unless we also feel responsibility for the needs of others, we are not really persons at all. This is the truth, as Christians see it, but we claim that it is really truth for everybody, for it has already received ample verification. There is good reason to think, then, that it applies to the industrial, the academic, and the political orders, and not merely to some fragment of life denoted the religious order.

One of the best contributions which Christian thought can

make to the thought of the world is the repetition of the reminder that life is complex. It is part of the Christian understanding of reality that all simplistic answers to basic questions are bound to be false. Over and over, the answer is *both-and* rather than *either-or*. The fact that there is validity in the appeal of individual liberty does not mean that there is any lack of validity in the appeal of the community. Only by keeping both in mind do we have a modicum of insurance against either anarchy or tyranny. The uninhibited libertarian is as much a menace as is the totalitarian, and vice versa. Modern democratic theory tends, unfortunately, to oscillate between two necessary ideals, each of which is valuable in conjunction but damaging in isolation. It is part of the vocation of the Christian intellectual to utter at least two warnings at once. There must be, on the one hand, a warning against any individualism which makes the separated person his own end; but there must be, at the same time, a warning against any collectivism which regards the community as the end of the individual.

Reprinted from *Quest for Reality,* InterVarsity Press, 1973.

12
Ethical Contagion

One of the most striking facts of the world is the fact of moral difference. Men differ from one another in a thousand ways, but all other differences fade into relative insignificance in comparison with differences in goodness. Though goodness is difficult to define, it is wonderfully easy to recognize. Often the difference is observable on first contact with another person, so radically do selfishness and greed, as well as their opposites, influence the whole man, even affecting his external appearance in many ways. This does not mean that the understanding of ethical problems is easy or simple, but it does mean that we know goodness when we see it, and to see it is a thrilling experience.

The paramount importance of goodness in human life becomes evident when we ask ourselves what kind of people we are willing to have as companions for long periods. For steady companionship it is sheer goodness that we prize most, providing we mean by goodness genuine excellence of character and not some trivial standard of conduct. The one whose companionship we prize is not the person who puts on a show of virtue for the sake of private gain, the self-centered man, or the man who would seek to use us for his own ends. Mere cleverness would finally become tiresome; dominating personalities are ridiculous after a time; humor we want in small doses; but goodness is permanently satisfying. Sometimes, indeed, we hear of people who are accused of being too good, but that merely indicates that these persons are superficially pious or are marked by an affectation of gentleness or generosity. When we think of the best people we know, we realize that they have something which cannot be overdone. The heart of goodness is *trustworthiness,* and there cannot be too much trustworthiness in the world.

In view of the fact that goodness is of paramount importance in the life of human beings, it is obvious that we should do all we can to learn how it is achieved or produced. There could be no more worthy task than that of discovering the conditions under which moral excellence arises, since the deliberate cultivation of these conditions might facilitate the development of the goodness we so greatly prize. We are tempted to conclude that goodness is born and that effort is therefore futile, but it is a fact that character can be changed. It is not surprising, therefore, that some of the best thought of great and good men has been devoted to this problem since the rise of civilization.

Before attempting a positive answer it is worthwhile to note some of the conditions which are not sufficient, either separately or together, to produce moral excellence. Perhaps the most obvious one of these is *wealth.* Money does not make men good and neither does poverty, inasmuch as we find all degrees of goodness combined with all degrees of economic standing. Rare beauty of character sometimes flourishes in city slums, but it is also found in homes of millionaires.

Socrates was a poor man of Athens, and Marcus Aurelius was the emperor of Rome with vast resources at his command, but both lived beautiful lives. In some sections of New York City the slum and the avenue are separated by only a few feet, but they are no closer geographically than they are morally. This is not to say that economic conditions have no bearing on the problem, but it does mean that they are not sufficient conditions. Certainly some conditions make goodness unusually difficult and these are chiefly the extreme conditions. The economic condition which presents the fewest hindrances to the development of goodness is one removed as far as possible from great wealth on the one hand and from dire poverty on the other.

Another condition which cannot account for goodness is *educa-*

tion. As in the case of wealth, it can be truly said that all degrees of goodness are actually combined with all degrees of training. Some moral giants have been rude, unlettered persons. The conspicuous example is that of the first apostles, Galilean fishermen. Almost everyone is acquainted with some genuine saint, usually of restricted circumstances, who may have read only a few books in his life. The best person I have ever known never went to college. On the other hand, there sometimes develops in educated circles a spirit of jealousy and struggle for personal power that makes us profoundly discouraged. Goodness is clearly much deeper than mere learning.

This holds in moral education as well as in strictly secular education. It is possible to study the moral standards of different peoples and argue endlessly about competing ethical theories without being made one whit better. Ethical scholarship and personal goodness are two different things.

In the same way we can say that a man's *profession* is not a sufficient condition of moral excellence. There seem to be good men in every kind of work and disgusting men in every kind of work. It is possible that some tasks make goodness easier, especially those which involve contact with the soil or which provide some physical work without the labor which exhausts. For example, gardeners often seem to have a high degree of what we most prize in men. At the same time there are tasks which are not consistent with moral dignity at all, particularly those by means of which some men are parasites. How nearly independent goodness is of profession is especially clear when we realize that participation in the ministry is no guarantee of goodness. In spite of pious words, and an unctuous manner, there are clergymen who, by a realistic test, are evil men. Churches are often scenes of bickering and bitterness. We can say, then, that occupation bears on the question, but is a minor consideration.

Another possible condition is that of beautiful *physical surroundings.* Some men live their entire lives in the presence of physical ugliness and filth, whereas others are in the presence of mountain lakes or carefully tended parks and lawns. It is very hard to see how goodness can ever come to flower in the sordidness of the average mining village, where flimsy houses are crowded together on a narrow street and where the only view is obstructed by a pile of slag. But the miracle does happen. At the same time persons surrounded by great beauty may be far from good.

When I began my teaching career I lived in North Carolina in a section which commanded a fine view of some mountains which were the first outposts of the Appalachian Range. It became my habit to look at these mountains daily, and I often thought how fine it would be to live among them. The people on those slopes, I said to myself, could hardly fail to be grand people, considering their surroundings. Later I visited the people who lived there and found that, for the most part, they were quite unaffected by the beauty about them. Indeed, most of them seemed unaware of the beauty, and there were evidences on every hand of moral decay. I went home knowing that physical beauty of surroundings, while it may help, is certainly not enough.

What, then, is enough? There is no perfect recipe in the sense that we can be completely sure of our results, but there is a great deal of accumulated wisdom on the subject; and, according to this wisdom, the prime conditions are two: *contagion* and *discipline.*

The *contagion* of goodness is well demonstrated in the experience of the apostles who, in spite of conspicuous limitations in other ways, became good men chiefly as a result of their acquaintance with Christ. We often use the word contagion only for what is evil, but the truth is that goodness is like a disease which must be caught from another who has it. Fortunately, however, the contact need not be direct in order to be efficacious. Thus goodness can be contagious at long range, and the life of Christ may have an effect on men today much like the effect it had on Peter and John. Goodness has about it an inherent attractiveness that is far more effective than all the arguments in the world. One example may be worth a thousand commands. This is another way of saying that goodness is really unique and that goodness is the only thing which will produce goodness.

If this is true we should act accordingly and try to provide for ourselves the constant opportunity of contagion. You cannot make yourself catch a germ, but you can at least place yourself where the germs are. So act that you bring yourself in steady contact with the highest excellence you know, for the soul grows by what it touches.

The *discipline* of goodness is only a special application of the principles of contagion and suggests the steady control which is necessary. When men do not respond to goodness it is because they are not sufficiently sensitive themselves to be helped by it. We need discipline to break down the barriers which hinder contagion. Back of anything that is really well done there is usually a long period of self-mastery which has so refined the powers that they seem to act spontaneously. It is well known that good "extempore" speakers are those who have made the most painstaking preparation. Perhaps they have not prepared the individual speech, but they have prepared the long background of the speech. Is it reasonable to suppose that excellence in character needs no discipline, when excellence in speaking needs so much?

The discipline for each task must be one appropriate to it. The appropriate discipline for the opening of our lives to the contagion of goodness is that which comes from times of personal quietness when we refuse to let our minds run hither and yon in a lazy fashion and hold them steadily to high things. The habitual practice of public as well as private prayer, not when we feel like it but with complete regularity, is comparable to the discipline of the musician who forces himself to practice in season and out.

Logan Pearsall Smith has put us in his debt by telling how Whistler learned to paint. The final painting in each case took an incredibly brief time; but before the final painting, literally hun-

dreds of others, of the same subject, were made and discarded. He
painted with speed, but it was long discipline that made the speed
possible. We see the successful last effort and tend to forget what
preceded it. It doesn't take much effort or time to do anything if
you know how, but it usually takes a long time to learn. It doesn't
take long to throw a javelin, but days of training are what makes
the throw good.

By the same token, goodness is difficult; and there is no royal
road to character. But there is a road, and a road which men are
at liberty to choose. That road is one in which we place our lives
in contact with contagious goodness and so discipline our spirits
that we are able to profit by the experience.

Reprinted from *Best Sermons,* Thomas Y. Crowell, 1959, pp. 149-154, with
the title "What Makes Men Good."

13
The Spiritual Dimension
of Inflation

The problem of inflation, which is one of the most serious of our generation, is essentially moral rather than merely financial. If we continue on the road on which we are now traveling, it is certain that we shall cheat our children, perhaps in a fashion that is irreparably damaging. Thoughtful people, including Christian people, need to think about this problem and to face it with deep seriousness.

If the present course is followed, with a comparable increase in governmental expenditure, the ultimate damage will be almost inconceivable. In the recent past, our national budget has been multiplied by five, advancing, in about twelve years, from one hundred to five hundred billion dollars. If the rate of increase remains the same, the annual budget will, in another twelve years, reach twenty-five hundred billion, the awful truth being that, unless there is a change in policy, this is precisely what will occur. It takes only a modest amount of logical thinking to realize that such a radical increase will produce runaway inflation, the dreadful thought being that it may be as bad as it was once in Germany, when a loaf of bread finally cost ten thousand marks.

It is the human cost of runaway inflation that is so terrible to contemplate. People who have sacrificed, in order to establish savings accounts, will be hardest hit, especially if they try to survive on fixed incomes, and life insurance will become practically worthless. The persons who suffer most, in such inflation, are the very ones who have been most careful in living within their incomes.

The ordinary citizen may be helped to understand how desperate the situation is by contemplating the purchase of a certificate of deposit. If the duration is for one year, the purchaser is promised 6 percent interest, but with inflation now at least 7 percent, he will actually have less at the end of the year than he had at the beginning, with a further loss of value because the interest earned is subject to income tax. Consequently, there is no way in which one who saves carefully can get ahead or even stay even. This is, indeed, a dismal prospect!

It is not scare talk to say that we are in a time when we are making decisions which may destroy our Republic, for it is realism to remind ourselves that catastrophic changes often come in situations which are now predictable. We all know that the economic disaster in Germany fifty years ago paved the way for the Nazi revolution which followed. When everything goes to pieces, people are sometimes willing to accept a strong though evil leader because he promises to make a new start. It is frightening to think what may be in store for ourselves.

Because each of us is a voter, each can influence the outcome by the ballot. We can let it be known that a governmental deficit of over $60 billion is really intolerable! With genuine moral firmness this could be eliminated entirely, for, as everyone knows, it includes a vast amount of sheer waste. The anti-inflation talk of many Congressmen is pure posturing, if they continually add to the deficit by trading expensive local projects for local votes. Though deficit spending may be justifiable in the bottom of a depression, this device, in a time of general affluence, reveals only lack of courage, since to accede to each demand for higher incomes rather than to hold the line is the easy response. Congressmen are especially vulnerable to this temptation when they desire reelection, only a profound ethical commitment being strong enough to enable them to resist such pressure.

Ordinary hardworking people do not know how opulent some of their public servants really are. Many would be shocked if they should learn of the double-dipping out of the common treasury by those who enjoy both lavish pensions and contemporary government salaries. For example, a colonel with thirty years of service can look forward, in a normal life span, to collecting $590,072.00. This does not include Social Security and may be increased by other payments. As our bureaucracy grows, both in number and in level of payment, a large part of our total public budget is that which pays those who are rendering no present service of any kind. The public does not seem to be aware of how heavy this burden has already become.

Each congressman and senator whom we elect costs us a fantastic amount. Though we are usually aware of the part of this which is actual salary, because it is published, we are less informed about the costs involved in the payment of staffs, and numerous journeys abroad, some of which have, at best, a marginal connection with recognized legislative duties. Only a small part of the corruption is actually illegal, but there are expenditures which, though not illegal, are unethical.

Other fat salaries in the private sector do harm in that they stir up dissatisfaction among modest people and thereby increase the upward pressure. The ridiculously inflated salaries of some television announcers and baseball players have been uniformly damaging in this regard. People know, in a dim way, that inflated incomes tend to be self-defeating, in that prices go up accordingly, but each one tries to get there first, anyway. The very idea of personal discipline in spending seems quaint!

The most dangerous feature of our situation is that of the mood of our people. Having some hint of the way things are going, the tendency on the part of the majority is to get on the bandwagon before it is too late. Each one who thus attempts to enrich himself is doing so at the expense of the total society.

Somewhere there must be a people who demonstrate the courage of nonconformity. Somewhere there must be those who, because of personal commitment, work for the sake of a cause rather than primarily for private gain. Strange as it may seem, there are still persons who willingly accept lower incomes in order to be able to participate in work that is intrinsically worthwhile. Some colleges have been made great by the self-denying devotion of professors who could have earned far more in other institutions, but who have continued their work in a spirit of unselfish dedication. As we examine the scene carefully, we soon realize that such devotion is more likely to appear in a religious setting than anywhere else. Ordinarily only something as strong as Christian commitment can give people the courage to oppose a general trend in the direction of self-indulgence.

What is there that committed Christians can do? They can make their concern known and thus help to change the climate of opinion. Personally, each of us can resist the temptation to engage in an ostentatious manner of living, personal austerity thus providing a model of the way in which our nation must go if disaster is to be avoided. Each one can resist personally the tendency to live ever more expensively.

If the above reasoning is correct, those who are committed Christians may be seen as playing a much larger role than they are generally supposed to play. Because Christianity exists, not for its own sake, but for the sake of the world, the nation as a whole has an immense stake in the health of the Christian community. Just as the economic problems turn out, upon analysis, to be fundamentally ethical ones, so the ethical renewal that is required turns out to be fundamentally spiritual, for that is where the power resides.

First published as a *Quarterly Yoke Letter,* June 1978.

14
The Essential Christian Unit

Anyone who undertakes to engage in a serious study of the teachings of Christ on prayer is likely to be surprised. One surprise comes in the clear account of what it is for which we ought, primarily, to pray, "Pray therefore the Lord of the harvest to send out laborers into his harvest" (Matt. 9:37; Luke 10:2, RSV). The fact that the identical admonition appears in two separated contexts makes it reasonable to conclude that Christ may have stressed the same point on many occasions. The importance of the particular injunction lies in the way in which it indicates what the primary strategy of the kingdom of Christ is. Fortunately, this conception is not alien to the minds of most of those who read this Letter, however unfamiliar it may be to millions. The greatest single contribution of the Yoke Movement has been the recognition that Christianity exists for workers, in that the yoke is a symbol of toil. The essential unit of the Christian faith is, we believe, the *work force!*

We understand how revolutionary this idea is when we contrast it with what preceded it in the biblical heritage. As we read 2 Chronicles we soon understand that the central interest of Solomon and those around him, so far as their religion was concerned, was the erection of a glorious building, which is accordingly described in minute detail. The major emphasis is upon an adequate ceremonial setting, the entire building being a place of incense. The greatest of the prophets went far beyond this notation. Their convictions reach a climax in the words of Micah: "He hath shown thee, O man, what is good; and what doth the Lord require of thee, but to do justly, and to love mercy, and to walk humbly with thy God?" (Mic. 6:8). In my own Bible, given to me after my father's death nearly forty years ago, my mother wrote in the margin opposite Micah 6:8, "Your father's favorite." What we have in the teaching of Christ is the logical conclusion of this development, proceeding from the merely ceremonial to the moral and spiritual.

If we try to envisage Christ's purpose, we come to realize that the essential unit of Christian endeavor is not the congregation of worshippers, valuable as they may be, and not the denomination, essential as that may be in organization, but the small group dedicated to the task of making a difference in the practical world. Christ leads us beyond the temple, and even beyond the synagogue, by drawing together and training a conscious work force.

Recently, in the experience of lying in the hospital bed with a fractured hip, I have been fortunate in being able to concentrate my thought for many days upon this important subject of what the basic Christian unit is or ought to be. In order to understand it better, I have tried to see if I could note any sequence in Christ's use of metaphors. First of all, I concentrated on the idea of the plow, which we find in Luke 9:62. I was helped in this regard by remembering how my dear friends of the Men's Movement in the old United Presbyterian Church made a lapel symbol in the shape of a walking plow, and wore it as a witness to the world. Indeed, I attended one of their conventions almost a quarter of a century ago and was impressed by the fact that nearly every person present displayed this symbol of work. Attenders kept saying to one another that anyone who puts his hand to the plow and looks back is not fit for the kingdom. Hundreds at that time came to see with great vividness that the basic unit of the Christian faith is not people who are visiting a shrine, or a crowd of persons making up an audience for a speaker, but is, instead, a group of laborers engaged in the harvesting task of reaching their perplexed and seeking brethren with something so vital that, if it is received, it will change their lives.

Meditation on the significance of the plow leads naturally to the emphasis upon the harvest, which Christ makes at more than one point in the gospel record. The plowing of the land in the early part of the season is justified by the equally hard work of reaping, which comes later. Christians are thus called not only to be plowmen, but also harvesters.

The harvest in which we are called to operate is the human one. All around us are people who are puzzled and confused, and this is true even of many who are nominal members of congregations. That the people indeed are like sheep without a shepherd is verified by the way in which they now are attracted by faddish developments, some of which have no substance at all. The spiritual hunger is so great that people will reach for that which is not really nourishing. I find it helpful, in this connection, to note the context in which the first reference to the call for harvesters appears, namely that of Matthew 9:36. Christ's call for harvesters is made because the human need is so obvious.

The emphasis which you and I have made upon the wearing of Christ's yoke needs now to be enriched by emphasizing the particular vocation of *Harvester*. We wear the yoke both to plow and to reap, but it is the reaping which needs most to be stressed at this time. We do well to remember the words of Christ: "Do you not say 'There are yet four months, then comes the harvest'? I tell you, Lift up your eyes, and see how the fields are already white for harvest" (John 4:35). This striking approach is brought to a climactic close in the trenchant words, "I sent you to reap" (John 4:38). The contemporary appropriateness of these words cannot be overemphasized.

What I wish to do in this particular letter is to share with all who are willing to read it my dream of the concrete character of a Christian work force in our generation. If you wish to be a part of this, as I think you do, you must understand that the price is very high! It is not possible to be a reaper in the present crisis of spiritual need unless certain abilities are consciously developed. Of these, three are now paramount: We must learn to *think;* we must learn to *speak;* we must learn to *write.* All of us know that a person's best message is proclaimed by his deeds, but we also know that action is not sufficient without appropriate words. As we approach seekers, our thinking must be so clear that, far from adding to the confusion, we bring some clarity to puzzled minds. Because the spoken word can sometimes make a real difference in people's lives, you and I must learn to speak well and to watch for opportunities to give the right message. Some opportunities may come, not merely in religious gatherings, but in various kinds of secular societies. Many who read these words should develop their powers in such a way that they can put in written form messages that are convincing, some of them in the form of personal letters. Such skill does not come with ease, but must be developed by constant toil.

The present spiritual situation is paradoxical in the extreme. On the one hand we cannot fail to be aware of the decline of the well-established denominations, several of them having fewer members each succeeding year. At the same time, however, we have a striking surplus of clergymen, many of whom desire pastorates, but cannot find them. When we observe the intensity of the seeking among the general populace, we conclude that people are indeed like sheep without a shepherd (Matt. 9:36). But the shortage is not that of clergy! It must, therefore, be in the rank and file of ordinary Christian women and men who are either not aware of the nature of their vocation or who are not prepared to carry it to fulfillment. It is still true, as it was in Milton's day, that "The hungry Sheep look up, and are not fed," but these words are now coming to have a new significance. It is still true, as Jesus said, that the laborers are few, for harvesting Christians are clearly a minority. Our central task, therefore, is to try to alter this sorrowful situation.

First published as a *Quarterly Yoke Letter,* September 1978.

15
The Wisdom of Paradox

That ours is a time of striking paradox no thoughtful person denies or even doubts. We have reasons for sorrow and reasons for rejoicing, and we have them mixed together. For many of us the month of December is a recurring symbol of the paradox, in that, on the one hand, it includes the shortest and darkest days of the year, while, on the other, it reminds us of the coming into history of the Light that "lighteth every man" (John 1:9).

Of all the paradoxical aspects of the current scene, nothing is more revealing than the phrase now beginning to achieve currency, "Religion up; morality down." A Dutch telecaster visiting America shocked many of his listeners when he asked how it is possible for there to be so many born-again Christians and yet for our society to be so sick. We may not know how to answer the visitor's penetrating question; but in any case, we dare not avoid it. We must look at our world with open eyes.

There is no need, in this particular essay, to stress the evidences of our moral sickness, for we see them every day. If, lacking courage to make hard decisions, we allow inflation to become a runaway phenomenon, the consequent harm to good and innocent people living on fixed incomes is terrible to contemplate. Whatever else can be said of the Christian who understands the meaning of the gospel, he is never an easy optimist. He knows that, however wide the door of opportunity may be, there are always "many adversaries" (1 Cor. 16:9). The simple answers are always wrong.

While never denying the prevalent moral sickness, the time comes when the primary need is for mutual encouragement, which is the purpose of this particular Letter. It is part of the total truth that, in the midst of the discouragement, there are signs of hope to which we can point and to which we ought to point. One such sign is the emergence of strong young Christian intellectuals. Because of my personal contact with these, both directly and by correspondence, I am deeply encouraged. Never, in my entire public life, have I been aware of so many young leaders who combine the warm heart and the clear head. Many of these are just under thirty years of age, with the consequent promise of many years of effective service when those of us who are of mature years will be gone from the scene.

There are individual congregations in which, though nothing that occurs will create news headlines, the reason for hope is genuine. I have just received a letter from a local pastor whose work I have observed for the past eight years and of whose purposes I am aware. He writes to say that, while nothing spectacular is occurring in the life of the congregation, he can point to thirty people who have accepted a common discipline and to five or six who demonstrate radically changed lives. Modest as his claim was, I nearly shouted when I read the pastor's letter. What he reported was the creation of the kind of conscious minority that gives us the best hope of changing the world.

The emphasis upon the voluntary acceptance of discipline requires amplification. It is this which Yokefellows have stressed from the beginning and which we must never cease to stress. Nearly every one who receives this Letter has signed a small card, undertaking faithfully to follow such disciplines as daily prayer, daily Scripture, regular worship, proportionate giving, and serious study. As a Christian order we are marked, not by a special garb or by a particular creed, but by the attempt to take Christ's yoke in such a way that we live truly disciplined lives.

The growth of the number who accept voluntarily a Christian discipline, in contrast to the popular conception of empty self-indulgent and egocentric freedom, is truly a sign of hope. One evidence of this development is the publication this year, by Harper & Row, of a valuable new book, *Celebration of Discipline.* This book, written by Richard J. Foster of Oregon, is the best contemporary study we know of the case for a disciplined life. Even the title is significant, in that it helps to counter the popular notion that a disciplined life is a somber one. The truly disciplined person not only has joy as a consequence of his way of life; he is much more effective than he could be otherwise. For example, the person who understands and practices the discipline of time has far more time to use than would be the case if he merely muddled along, without conscious order.

Another sign of Christian hope is the evidence of the renewed effectiveness of adult education. The success of the Yokefellow Academy in recruiting and training thousands of serious students, chiefly within churches, is not really exceptional, for similar efforts are appearing in various areas. Earlier this autumn I shared personally in a Christian school in Georgia, with one thousand persons registered. The excitement experienced by mature persons discovering the joys of study for the first time in their lives is a moving sight.

In a few communities there has been introduced, within congregations, the scholarly study of the Greek language. Mature people are thrilled to realize that there is nothing to hinder their developing the ability to read the New Testament in the language in which it was written. The more we think about it, the more absurd it seems to suppose that such studies should be limited to the very young. One middle-aged woman, with whose work I am familiar, is now engaged in a thorough study of logic and is clearly loving it, in spite of the difficulty of the task.

The most encouraging development with which I am acquainted is that of the creation in the local congregation of a "work force." In one congregation this group is known as "The Seventy," the language employed deriving from the tenth chapter of Luke. The originators are conscious of Christ's request that his followers pray for the emergence of such a force. "Pray therefore the Lord of the harvest to send out laborers into his harvest" (Luke 10:2). In one local church the pastor sees his nourishment of the "Valiant Seventy" as his central responsibility. He defends this allocation of his time and energy because he sees powerful minorities as our best hope for changing the character of the world. Only in this way, he believes, can the statement "Religion Up; Morality Down" be made obsolete.

Though the contemporary church is weak and ineffective at many points, there is clearly a new emphasis upon the redemptive power of fellowship. Whatever else we know or do not know, we are at least aware that individual religion is largely ineffective. Only as we rediscover the significance of the New Testament phrase "one another" are we likely to make a genuine or an enduring difference. Only as we are yoked together are we truly instruments of the kingdom of Christ.

There is always a danger that we may think of ourselves as links in a chain. The trouble with a chain is that it is no stronger than its weakest link. If one is broken, all is consequently ineffective. The Christian idea is a radically different one. We are called, not to be part of a chain, but strands of cable, in which many elements, individually weak, are strong together, because each helps to strengthen other strands and consequently the whole cable. If you are now helping, anywhere, to create a fellowship, you are one of the signs of hope.

First published as a *Quarterly Yoke Letter*, December 1978.

16
The Jonestown Tragedy

When, in November 1978, news of the Jonestown tragedy reached the general public, a common reaction was one of puzzlement verging on disbelief. How, it was repeatedly asked, could such an event occur? How could it be that hundreds of Americans would engage in mass suicide and murder, at the command of the leader of their supposedly ideal community?

Now, looking back at the tragedy from the vantage point of elapsed time, we can see that the sense of mystification, once so widespread, was almost entirely wrong. As we think more carefully we see that the disastrous event in South America, far from being mysterious, was the logical outcome of a development which had already taken place in Indiana and California. The right understanding of this development is extremely important for all who care about the survival of our civilization, and particularly for those who face the future from a Christian perspective.

The steady movement toward disaster is best understood when we realize that the story is one of general *uprootedness*. Many of those who died were the "Flower Children," liberated, as they supposed, from the moral standards of the local communities from which they had fled. For many of these for whom there was no real sense of meaning, the first reaction was a feeling of liberation. For a while they rejoiced in their empty freedom, which included sexual promiscuity and the drug culture; but this was a position which, in the nature of events, could not be long maintained. Spiritually hungry, they looked for sustenance, and it appeared to them that they had found it in the leadership of the man who had started life in Randolph County, Indiana. The empty house, as

Christ taught us, cannot remain empty. The effort to maintain a spiritual vacuum permanently is literally impossible.

Because Christ's parable of the empty house is not well remembered or even widely understood, it is worthwhile to repeat it here. The parable is preserved for us in both Matthew and Luke, the Lucan version being as follows: "When the unclean spirit has gone out of a man, he passes through waterless places seeking rest; and finding none he says, 'I will return to my house from which I came.' And when he comes he finds it swept and put in order. Then he goes and brings seven other spirits more evil than himself, and they enter and dwell there; and the last state of that man becomes worse than the first" (Luke 11:24-26).

If we did not realize it before, we know now that people whose lives are meaningless will *grasp* for a meaning and will, in many instances, accept it uncritically. The counterculture is restless without an answer. It is important for us to try to see why Jim Jones appeared to have an answer to the needs of the spiritually uprooted. We need to understand partly because we can be sure that the Jonestown tragedy is not the last of its kind. If enough of our generation understand, some calamities may, however, be avoided.

Part of the initial puzzlement in the general public arose from misunderstandings. Many supposed, for example, that the People's Temple was a church, in the ordinary sense of the word, and that James Jones was an avowed Christian. Both suppositions were false. Furthermore, many thought of the settlement in South America as an agricultural mission, similar to the missions which many of us support by our giving. It was naturally supposed that the settlement had been established to lift the economic and spiritual level of the surrounding population. It was, by contrast, a *commune,* organized specifically to enable citizens to escape from the problems of North American culture.

Though he began as a Christian, James Jones moved farther and farther to the left, so that he soon became a Marxist, accepting the totalitarianism which Marxism necessitates. Indeed, the South American scene was a frankly temporary abode, with the U.S.S.R. as the ultimate destination. What began as a flaming idealism, especially in regard to race and poverty, led, by its own dialectic, to acceptance of the necessity of tyranny, in order to make the idealism secure. Absolute freedom, which carries within itself the means of its own destruction, led, by irreversible steps, to the abolition of freedom.

The whole story shows how vulnerable and inconsistent the popular philosophy is. If, as so many claim to believe, there is no real right, but only the passing "preferences" of finite men and women, what reason is there to claim that Jones was wrong? According to this popular philosophy, the critics of Jones do what they like to do, and Jones did what he liked. If he liked personal power and adulation of obedient followers, what is wrong with that? If there's nothing good or bad but thinking makes it so, by what standard can the dictated suicide be criticized?

The debacle cannot be understood unless we realize that James Jones began as what we normally call an orthodox liberal. So much was he a part of the liberal establishment that he was given public office by the government of all of the cities in which he lived. He was known as a friend of the poor, a vigorous upholder of civil rights, a staunch champion of racial justice. In this crusader role, he was able to deliver a large bloc of votes to the party of his choice.

One key to an understanding of the complex situation is the recognition, in the Jones philosophy, of a clear separation between social ethics and personal ethics. Very firm in regard to race, he was conspicuously infirm in regard to sex. Indeed, he acknowledged the fatherhood of a child of one of his female followers. Matters of moral integrity were trivial compared with matters of social justice. This helps us to see why even murder could be logically condoned because individual life seems unimportant in the effort to achieve an ideal social order.

Enough time has elapsed since the November holocaust to allow us to see it in some intellectual perspective. We can look at it more calmly now than was possible at first, and we can see that the root of the problem is philosophical. Jones and his followers were religious, not in the sense of belief in Almighty God, but in the sense of absolute commitment to a cause. This involves absolute obedience to the leader's command whenever the Marxist ideal is supposed to be at stake. In short, what we have observed, to our horror, is not lack of faith, but far too much faith. What is so pathetic is that all of the actors in the terrible drama seem to have supposed that they were doing something noble. These pathetic people clearly thought that they were dying for a cause.

The mass suicide in Guyanna is the gruesome conclusion of the saga of the flower children. The cut flowers *did* wither. Cut off from the complex of social influences of home, church, family doctor, aunts and uncles, where could they go? They fled to a minor dictator and to death. As always occurs, the drift to extreme socialism led straight to a new tyranny. If people are absolutely uprooted they soon become easy targets for the claims of new messiahs.

What occurred in a South American jungle on November 18, 1978, should serve as a powerful warning to every thoughtful person that our responsibility is to bring meaning to as many lives as possible before it is too late. We have good reason to suppose that one means of doing this is the promulgation of the total gospel of Jesus Christ.

First published as a *Quarterly Yoke Letter,* March 1979.

17
What Time It Is

One of my greatest fears about our generation is the fear that we may not know what time it is. If we do not know the time, it is very likely that our efforts, however sincere, will be wasted. There is, for example, little value in trying to answer questions which people are not really asking.

Of the Gospel writers, Luke seems to have had the keenest sense of the importance of knowing the time. His memorable and sorrowful sentence on the subject (Luke 19:44) is unique to his Gospel, the others seeming to have missed it or have failed to see its significance. In the brilliant translation of *The New English Bible* the sentence reads, "You did not recognize God's moment when it came." The shocking fact is that most of Christ's contemporaries did not recognize him at all. The priests went on with their temple ritual, without any hint that there was One among them who had already made their obsessive interests obsolete. Pilate, the local representative of the imperial government, was slightly disturbed; but his disturbance was not sufficient to make a difference in his final action. Partly out of cowardice, Pilate missed the one great chance of his life.

As we try to understand the particular time in which we now live, we face two opposite dangers, complacency and despair. Because the time is *mixed,* those who follow either of these are seriously mistaken in judgment. It is a mistake, in the first place, to conclude that our society is fundamentally so sound that we are bound to come out all right. The trouble with such an optimistic stance is that it is based on false assumptions. It is like saying "Peace, peace," when there is no peace (Jer. 6:14; 8:11).

That the rosy view is a false one is perfectly clear when we look seriously at inflation. Unless we solve the problem of inflation, much of which is more moral than economic in origin, our society will go to pieces. It is an important fact of history that inflation has, in the past, pulled down the world's leading nations. The awful thing about our current inflation, which is damaging to our basic values, is that it is still increasing. So long as the overwhelming desire of each segment of society is to get its own, the problem will not be solved at all, but will instead become worse.

Along with inflation there goes general increase in crime and marked decrease in the strength of the family. One of the most shocking of revelations about the family is the fact that, in widely publicized court trials which involve men and women living together without marriage, the major question is whether there has been a "contract." When the emphasis is on contract we are being told, in no uncertain terms, that the Christian values have not only been abandoned, but are not even *understood.* In the Christian concept of the family, the emphasis is not upon a contractural relation, but upon a *commitment.*

We know a great deal about Christian values when we understand that a woman and a man take each other "for better, for worse, for richer, for poorer," the question of how much each earns being totally irrelevant. The sorrow is that, for many in our generation, this conception is merely quaint. Furthermore, there are millions, in the contemporary scene, who do not understand the Christian idea that private or secret marriage is a contradiction in terms. Christians have always believed that marriage must be public, the vows of lifelong fidelity being witnessed by the members of the caring community. What is shocking about our time is that there are so many who have never even heard of this truly revolutionary idea.

Part of the required realism in our time is the frank recognition of how scheming persons can make religion into a racket. The fact that so many of our neighbors are living under a sense of strain

makes religious racketeering particularly easy today. Though it seems almost unbelievable, it is a fact that one who claims to represent Christ's cause has boasted, in a television broadcast, that his religious income is nearly $300,000 annually. It is not surprising that people who are already disenchanted with all public figures jump to the conclusion that the church is as bad as the world. When we realize that religion can be part of the problem, rather than the answer, we realize that a sentimental optimism is an unsupportable position.

If sentimental optimism is mistaken, the mood of despair is equally so. There are many reasons why we must never adopt the position of hopelessness, the most important being that this is God's world. If Christ is trustworthy, God has not given up on his people and will never give up, however foolish we prove ourselves to be. A second convincing reason for rejecting despair is that there are evidences of faithfulness, providing we are wise enough to see them. In short, the apparently dominant paganism, far from being universal in scope, is actually challenged at important points. There are couples who understand the meaning of marriage and who are faithful in their mutual commitment. Even in colleges there are students who are nonconformists, so far as the surrounding paganism is concerned, some having the courage to uphold chastity.

Even though many churches are dull and disappointing, simply going through the motions and appearing to be spiritually empty, there are local congregations which demonstrate genuine vitality. There are spiritual leaders who personally resist the growing tendency to expect high salaries and who give their services with little or no thought of reward. How many of these there are, we do not know, but knowing *some* is sufficient to provide an antidote to despair.

In the leadership of the Christian cause, there is really more hope among amateurs than among the professionals. This is particularly evident among Christian women who may give us much

of the needed intellectual leadership of our generation. The challenge to women to become Christian intellectuals is being taken seriously by some of the best feminine minds. That this is really fresh and new is obvious when we realize that nearly all of the theology of the past has been produced by men. In short, there is light in the midst of the darkness.

Remember that Christian philosophy has nearly always been couched in paradox. This has been particularly true since the time of Blaise Pascal, who, more than three hundred years ago, taught us, in his valuable fragments of thinking, to see that the single truth is never adequate, because the world is never simple. "There is a God whom men can know, and there is a corruption in their nature which renders them unworthy of Him." We are false when we recognize only the light, and we are equally false when we recognize only the darkness. Error is truth separated from its balancing counterpart.

If there is one message I wish to give to my generation, it is that which appears in the brilliant translation which Dr. J. B. Phillips has made of John 1:5: "The light still shines in the darkness and the darkness has never put it out."

First published as a *Quarterly Yoke Letter*, June 1979.

18
Life in Britain

Word has reached me from some of my correspondents that I ought to devote this particular essay to some account of a stay in Great Britain in the early summer of this year. This request seems to me a reasonable one because the cultural and spiritual ties between the British and American peoples are so close. Historically it has been true that developments which appear first in Britain appear later in North America. Personally, moreover, the ties are very close for me. Recently, in London, I was deeply moved at the thought of the courage of John and Agnes Trueblood as they set sail, in 1682, from London, for a land of which they knew almost nothing and from which they were destined never to return.

Externally, the most shocking fact of England is that its inflation is even worse than ours. Indeed we soon realized, this summer, that nearly all prices are double of those of four years ago, when we paid an earlier visit to London. It is not uncommon, for example, for a tourist to be forced to pay sixty dollars a night in a hotel. Though the local people do not, for the most, use hotels, they nevertheless face inflated prices for food, clothing, and transportation. It is really hard to see how the poor are able to survive at all, yet the shops on Oxford Street are crowded from morning to night. And, on the whole, the people seem cheerful.

The spiritual life represents a genuine paradox. On the one hand, there are obviously far more church buildings than are required for efficient use, but the great cathedrals and Westminster Abbey are crowded all day long. St. Paul's Cathedral, the spiritual center of the British people, is constantly flanked by sight-seeing buses, and the turmoil inside Wren's magnificent building is similar to that of a busy railway station. Though the cathedrals outside London do not draw as many people as does St. Paul's, they, too, seem to have visitors all of the time. Our best examples of this phenomenon were York Minster, Durham Cathedral, and Chester Cathedral.

If we could know why people flock to the cathedrals, we might know something of real importance about the life of a people. Unfortunately, the great majority of attenders are not motivated primarily by the desire to worship Almighty God. Many, of course, gather in the mood normally associated with museums. We are bound to wonder if the crowds will still flock to Salisbury and Coventry if the time comes when the faith which inspired these magnificent structures is no longer seriously held by anybody. The probability is that the crowds will still gather, just as they gather on the Acropolis in Athens when the original purpose of the temples has been abandoned for nearly two thousand years. A modern test case is that of Russia. People still visit St. Isaac's Cathedral in Leningrad, but the mood is not identical with that which we sense at Canterbury or Wells.

The tourist mood in Britain, on the part of both residents and visitors, is nostalgic. Millions flock to Britain from overseas, thereby making the tourist industry highly profitable to the local economy; and they do so partly because of the reminders of greatness which are encountered on almost every side. Sitting, as long as I did a few weeks ago, in Poet's Corner of the Abbey, I often heard more German, French, and Japanese tongues than English. And no wonder! These people from far and near, disenchanted with their contemporary lives and leadership, are glad to be reminded of true greatness. Who can miss this as he remembers William Shakespeare, Samuel Johnson, and so many more? Even the unpoetic tourist from Sydney or Capetown or Toronto or Kokomo understands the deep significance of the lines which honor our American poet, T. S. Eliot, to the effect that the words of the dead are tongued with flame more than are the words of the living.

The spiritual experience just mentioned comes to focus for many, regardless of geographic location, when, in the floor at the west end of the Abbey nave, they read, "Remember Winston Churchill." There have been other great people in the twentieth century, in addition to Churchill, just as there were many brave men before Agamemnon, but most of them are forgotten. The tourists flock to the nine-hundred-year-old building in a kind of unconscious determination *not to forget*. The Dean of the Abbey is wise in bringing the great crowd to genuine silence every hour on the hour, for prayer. The connection with the supporting faith is not entirely severed, even though many of the church buildings are almost empty on Sunday mornings.

Britain is extremely fortunate in the preservation of its cathedrals, many of which are seven or eight centuries old. The modern person, long accustomed to the shoddy and the synthetic, may be truly lifted by looking at buildings put together with fidelity and precision hundreds of years ago. The sensitive observer is almost bound to contemplate the lives of our simple ancestors, many of whom could not read or write, but who could put cut stones on one another in a way that continues to this day.

What is more remarkable about the medieval cathedral builders is their evident motivation. They built carefully, slowly, artistically, not primarily for personal gain, but for the love of God. They were producing something of magnificence and enduring beauty, and they knew that they were doing so. There is a consequent determination, on the part of all but the most insensitive of moderns, to try to perform some equally noble task in this our own time. England is not the only country which possesses great cathedrals, but there is no other country in which cathedrals play a larger role in the spiritual life of a people.

I do not know and cannot know that I shall ever be in the land of my fathers again; but I do know that, for fifty-five years, the reminders of a cultural heritage have been important in the development of my own mind and career. I feel fortunate that once more, on May 24, I was able to walk up Aldersgate, as John Wesley did on that date in 1738. I pray that my heart may be as strangely and powerfully warmed as his heart was. I am pleased that, on May 16, I could walk on Great Russell Street, near the famous bookshop of Tom Davies in which Johnson and Boswell met. I know that, apart from the meeting of the young Scottish lawyer and the Great Cham of literature, the most famous of all biographies would never have been produced.

Contemporary contact with Britain is supremely important because of our manifest need of roots. If we have only the present we have almost nothing at all. Without a dynamic sense of the past we become superficial indeed. However bright contemporary flowers may be, they inevitably wither if they are severed from their spiritual roots. I have believed this for a long time, but now, as I return to the land which I love best, I believe it more than ever before. Whether modern civilization will survive, we cannot know, but we can be sure that survival will not be possible unless the conditions are met, for progress is never automatic. I love Britain partly because it teaches me what some of the conditions are.

First published as a *Quarterly Yoke Letter,* September 1979.

19
The Middle East

I sense, among my correspondents, real puzzlement about the Middle East. What are we to believe in the face of conflicting reports? The Holy Land is important to all of us, partly because it is the land of the Bible, the land where Jesus walked, but, even more, because of the threat to world peace which trouble in this area represents.

The perplexity which so many feel is increased by daily events. Many looked upon Israel, when its nationhood was established, in our time, as a fulfillment of prophecy; but when they see the extreme militarism of the new nation, they wonder. Many who were willing to envisage refugee camps of displaced persons as temporary expedients are deeply worried when they see gross injustice settling into a permanent condition. The continued establishment of illegal settlements on Arab land has increased anger more than any other single factor. The dream of a land in which people beat their swords into plowshares and their spears into pruning hooks, so that everyone can sit under his vine and figtree and none shall make them afraid (Mic. 4:3, 4), has not been realized at all. The repeated news reports of bombs planted in Israeli towns, or dropped from planes in Lebanon, sadden all of us.

My own effort to help my readers to form sound judgments about this perplexing problem has been aided by several visits to the area and by the direct reports of my former students who now teach there. I have also been greatly helped by the book *Search for Peace in the Middle East,* edited by my former colleague, Landrum Bolling. Unlike most studies of the problem, this valu-

119

able book rejects the temptation to take sides between the Jewish and Arab peoples. "On some issues, we believe," say the authors, "the Arabs have been clearly wrong and on other issues the Israelis have been clearly wrong." The honest Christian, whatever the emotional pressure from either side, is called to evenhandedness. This position, which is never really popular, is rendered especially difficult in the United States because of the activities of competing lobbies.

We are not likely to be helpful in facing the perplexing problem of the Middle East unless we start with some historical perspective. For fully two thousand years, after the Roman conquest, there was no Jewish state in Palestine. Jews, scattered over the world, particularly in European states, had no homeland. The conviction that they would never have political security without a government of their own led to the development of Zionism. During the First World War, the famous Lord Balfour, foreseeing the breakup of the Ottoman Empire, invited Jews to establish in Palestine a "National Home." The basic document of this radically new development, written in November 1917, appeared in the form of a letter addressed to the President of the English Zionist Federation, Lord Rothschild, signed by Balfour as British Foreign Secretary. This letter is what came to be widely known as the "Balfour Declaration." The name survived, even after the mandate of the League of Nations whereby Great Britain administered Palestine following the war.

The initiative of the Foreign Secretary opened the door for immigration of Jews to Palestine. Peacefully at first, and later by force or intimidation, the immigrants displaced many of the local Arabs whose ancestors had lived in the area for centuries. This is what has led to the fierce hatred which continues to this day. As early as 1925, when Balfour paid a visit to the area to open the Hebrew University on Mt. Scopus, the tension was already rising, particularly in adjoining states. One evidence of this was the anger aroused in Syria which led to Balfour's speedy withdrawal from that country.

In subsequent years the situation has worsened, leading to a succession of wars, in which the superiority of the military power of Israel has been demonstrated. The United Nations, which is the responsible body, in that it created the state of Israel, sought a just solution after the 1967 war between the Arab states and Israel. This is incorporated in the U.N. Resolution 242, which was accepted unanimously by the Security Council. The resolution calls upon Israel to withdraw from all the lands occupied in the 1967 war, which include the West Bank, the Gaza strip, East Jerusalem, the Golan Heights, and the Sinai. By means of the peace initiative of President Sadat of Egypt, the withdrawal from the Sinai is being largely accomplished; but there has been no withdrawal from the other places listed in the resolution.

The difficulty of the general problem is vastly increased now by the vulnerability of Lebanon and the local conflict there between Christians and Palestinian refugees. Beyond this lies the ever-present problem of oil, on which contemporary man has made himself dependent by the creation of modern engines. The Arabs have a near monopoly on the oil supply of the troubled area.

Granted that there is no quick or simple solution of a problem which has lasted so long and has aroused so much sense of injustice, it is nevertheless incumbent upon us to look for a longtime solution. What position can a thoughtful and caring contemporary Christian take?

In the first place, we must urge all parties to recognize Israel as a fact. It has not turned out precisely as Lord Balfour intended, but Israel is undoubtedly a nation and, though small, a powerful one. It is clearly here to stay. In the second place, the world must provide a homeland for the Palestinians just as it earlier provided a homeland for the Jews. To condemn human beings to permanent refugee status is morally intolerable. This is far more likely to occur if the Palestinians abjure terroristic tactics and rely on world goodwill which is manifestly growing, particularly in America. The Southern Christian Leadership has played a significant role in this new development, and for this we ought to be grateful. In the third place, we must reject, now and forever, the concept that military aggression is a justifiable ground for ownership of territory. No good society, anywhere, is possible with military occupation.

When we begin to understand both the antiquity and the complexity of the problems of the Middle East, we realize that there is no quick or simple solution. After so much pain and anger there may not be any really good solution, but, nevertheless we must try. In any case we can pray. Our prayer is that, somehow, the land where Jesus walked may become a place of both justice and peace.

First published as a *Quarterly Yoke Letter,* December 1979.

20
Church and State

The revolution in Iran, which has shaken people all over the world, is significant, partly because it represents one extreme answer to the perennial question of church and state. The answer so confidently given to the world by the Ayatollah Khomeini is that of a total rejection of any tension between religion and government. The tension is eliminated by the simple device of maintaining that the ecclesiastical and the political spheres are and *should be* identical in scope. The Ayatollah claims to have rejected all secularism and to have established a state that is completely dependent upon Moslem ideology. The basis of all law, therefore, is the divinely revealed Koran, and right and wrong are what the spiritual leaders say that it is.

That this simplistic solution of the problem of church and state is violently evil is obvious to the great majority of thinking persons. A problem is indeed solved, but the price of the solution is high. It is the price of the rejection of the freedom of the individual person. We do not have to be very wise to see that the Ayatollah's plan will eventually be rejected, however fanatical his following may now be. The clock cannot be turned back!

In strong contrast to Iran, the major danger of our western culture lies, not in the identification of religion and government, but at the opposite end of the spectrum, that is to say, in *total separation.* Very strong forces are at work to produce a system in which there is a total rejection of all religious influences. The drive in this direction is to be observed on many fronts, one of which is the practical elimination of religious influence from the public schools. The popular view is that prayer cannot be part of education. Part of the sorrow of our situation lies in the fact that those who would drive a wedge between religion and education have been remarkably successful, but their very success may be rationally seen as one of the causes of the manifest decline in the quality of the schools.

If the fanatical separatists could have their way, there would be no more connection between God and government in the United States than there is in Russia. The full taxation of church property is naturally one of the goals of those who are fanatically dedicated to separation of church and state.

Fortunately, the positions of the Iranians and of the American separatists do not exhaust the logical possibilities. There is a *third way!* What we seek and what we partly have in North America is a pattern of life equidistant from either theocracy or secularism. We seek a vision of wholeness in which all aspects of experience, including the political and governmental, are influenced by a positive and conscious spiritual ideal. We think, and with good reason, that the best life for mankind is that in which we act justly, love mercy, and walk humbly (Mic. 6:8); and we do not see much evidence that a purely secular state is likely to promote the ideals which the good life requires. Indeed, there is evidence that pure secularism leads normally to pagan self-aggrandizement. If people have no conviction that there is an objective moral order, rooted in the very being of Almighty God, the forces which inhibit self-interest are not likely to be sufficiently strong to produce a really good society. Even with all of the accumulated spiritual forces of history, we do a manifestly inadequate job; what would it be like if the spiritual influences should cease to operate entirely?

We do not want to have a nation dominated by any particular religion, and we do not want a nation which is independent of all religion. To get out of the gutter of ecclesiasticism is no gain if, as a consequence, we fall into the opposite gutter of sheer paganism. That is why we print on our money "In God We Trust" and adorn the walls of Congress with the same reverent words. We are thereby saying, in a most vivid fashion, that we dare not depend upon our own unaided powers. We know that we need all of the help that we can get. There are, of course, radicals who sneer at the famous motto, which was first adopted under the leadership of Abraham Lincoln, but we hope that those who sneer are never able to prevail.

The most solid barrier faced by those who seek to remake the United States of America into a purely secular state, without any reference to the will of Almighty God, is the Federal Thanksgiving. When they claim, as many do, that there is no legal connection between our government and the love of God, they are overlooking Thanksgiving Day. It is an important part of our history that, beginning with President Lincoln in 1863, every succeeding president has called this nation to an expression of prayer and gratitude. Anyone who overlooks this fact is not likely to understand the development of American culture. Here is something totally different from the continuation of some local colonial pattern. It is, instead, a declaration by the highest elected officer of the nation speaking to all, of every faith or no faith. It is, indeed, one of the most beautiful things that has occurred in our total history.

It brings a certain clarification of mind to try to see the distinction between Thanksgiving and Christmas. Christmas is chiefly for Christians, though not limited to them; but it was not instituted by government, whereas Thanksgiving has been. Christmas comes because Christ was born; Thanksgiving comes because Abraham Lincoln and all of his successors have perceived that *God can call a nation.* We may fail to respond to the call, but that is no evidence that we are not called.

At this point, a small addition to my autobiography may be in order. Fortunately, I attended a high school which, with no apology whatever, encouraged both excellence and reverence. The Christian commitment of our principal was well understood throughout the entire community. All of our assemblies began

with Scripture and prayer; and, on one afternoon a week, I attended, at the close of school, a meeting of the high school Y.M.C.A.
From this potent organization teams of young men were sent to
the surrounding towns, and I was one of those involved.

Was this a breaking of the wall of separation between church
and state? It most certainly was, and for that we can be grateful.
Moreover, the action of the devout principal accorded with the
wishes of the overwhelming majority of the citizens. Why should
they be denied such a boon? Was it a denial of the First Amendment to the Constitution of the United States? Most certainly not.
So far as denominations are concerned, there was no "establishment of religion." Our principal was indeed a Methodist, but there
was not even a hint of the establishment of Methodism. No student was forced to attend the meetings of the Y.M.C.A. and the
Y.W.C.A., and no one was made to feel like an outsider. I never
felt any pressure to conform.

As I have thought carefully about the matter in succeeding
years I have realized that, in our high school, we were being
faithful to the First Amendment, which, as is sometimes forgotten, has a positive as well as a negative emphasis. Congress, we are
told, shall make no law concerning religion which prohibits "the
free exercise thereof." Our beautiful assemblies, like our learning
of the Latin text of Christmas carols, were examples of "free
exercise." The notion that this was harmful to anyone else is so
preposterous that only a fanatic would take it seriously.

It is important to realize that those who now put great stress
on the separation of church and state, leading, in practice, to the
enthronement of a dogmatic atheism, are really proposing a radical alteration in the entire character of America. The burden of
proof is upon them, not upon the defenders of a noble heritage.

Modern Russia claims to be a wholly secularized state, just as
contemporary Iran claims to be totally Islamic. In Russia, the idea
of prayer in the Kremlin gatherings is unthinkable, while in Iran
the absence of prayer is equally unthinkable. We can be grateful

for the fact that we belong to a nation which, however numerous our failures may be, seeks a third way. We are glad that our Congress opens with prayer for divine guidance; we are glad that, at inaugurations, we still employ the Holy Bible; we are glad that we appoint chaplains in prisons and the armed forces. When there is such a wonderful middle way, it is strange that anyone opts for either gutter.

First published as a *Quarterly Yoke Letter,* March 1980.

21
The Last Chapter
of Life

The Christian faith, in its avowed catholicity, must always attempt to speak to the needs of all sorts and conditions of men. Though it must, therefore, minister to the young, it must, at the same time, minister to those who carry the burdens of middle years, and likewise to those who have entered into the evening of life. Partly because I am in it myself, I now have a special tenderness for those who are aware that they are involved in the last chapter of their lives. For the first time, the students whom I now address are my own contemporaries! I am glad, for their sakes, to affirm now what I wrote more than thirty years ago, in the Preface to *The Common Ventures of Life,* "The best life for mankind will always be that life in which the inevitable experiences are undertaken with the most intelligence, reverence, and courage." Just as death is inevitable for each of us, so is old age, unless there occurs the tragedy of early demise. Since old age normally cannot be avoided, the path of wisdom is to face it with expectancy.

The expectancy that is desired must be such that it is compatible with realism. By realism is meant the recognition that not all will be enjoyable or comfortable. There will, undoubtedly, be diminution of energy, some dimming of eyesight, and, for nearly all older persons, arthritic pain, the prevalence of such pain being indicated by the number of medications which are advertised for its relief. About all this there is, of course, nothing new. When Dr. Samuel Johnson wrote his noblest poem, *The Vanity of Human Wishes,* he referred to the kind of pain which is known to nearly all older people, regardless of race or sex, in the line "Unnumber'd maladies his joints invade." With this, millions can identify. When we say blithely with Robert Browning, "The best is yet to be," we run the risk of being gullible, unless we also face the dangers and difficulties of old age, without evasion. A visit to almost any nursing home should suffice to cure anyone of easy optimism. The last years of some people are simply dreadful! Once we are realistic about the physical dangers, we must also be realistic about the spiritual and moral dangers of longevity. Partly because the pains and disappointments are real, it is easy for persons of advanced years to engage in complaints and recrimination.

In spite of the obvious impediments of old age, there are also actual advantages which are to some degree compensatory. One significant compensation of age is freedom from hurry. Whereas, in most of our years, some degree of hurry is a necessity, even for survival, in the final years a slower pace is wholly practicable. It is a genuine blessing not to have to dress with speed or to fight the clock in trying to reach one's scene of employment. Much joy comes in doing the necessary tasks of life one at a time. It is especially pleasant not to be hectic in the effort to catch up with an overdemanding schedule.

A similar liberation of late maturity is freedom from ambition. For years, ambition to succeed in business or profession may be a driving urge, but the day comes when that pressure can be removed. The mature woman may rightly look neat, but she has no need to appear on each occasion in a new dress. Her task is to be a good person, not to make an impression. It is chiefly by being good persons ourselves that we help others, our very courage in the face of adversity giving others more assistance than we realize. Some of the noblest examples of human character appear when the drive for success has been outgrown.

One of the experiences of maturity which demonstrates the advantage of a slow pace is the opening of the daily mail. Often, in middle life, this is an essentially hectic task, in which we are forced to hurry if we are to keep promises in other operations. The consequence is that we miss potential richness. Ideally the opening and reading of letters can rightly be seen as a spiritual exercise because some friendships may be renewed thereby. Since we cannot know who our correspondents will be, each envelope may rightly be approached with excitement. Will I hear today from a person whose handwriting I have not seen for years? Will a message come from far away? Much as we complain about the inefficiency of the postal system, it is a fact that the daily mail may become sacramental in that it is "an actual conveyance of spiritual meaning and power by a material process."

The possibility of solitude is an advantage of later years which is often unnoted. Though, in most of our active days, we are surrounded by other people, the older person can, if he or she desires, spend much time alone, and thereby become a better person. One who has seen this clearly is the late Albert Einstein, who, toward the end of his life, wrote, "I live in that solitude which is painful to youth, but delicious in the years of maturity." The signal blessing of being allowed to be alone, without the necessity to impress, is something that can counterbalance many difficulties.

Though the spiritual life may be nurtured in all periods of our earthly pilgrimage, it can be nurtured in old age with increasing attention. The biblical injunction "Pray without ceasing" (1 Thess. 5:17), while not easily obeyed in the middle years, may actually become practicable as the end draws near. There are many for whom we ought to pray; and prayer can, finally, be just under the surface of consciousness all of the time. It may help each of us to know that some persons, in spite of their physical weakness, are praying for us now. One of the reasons why prayer is important to persons of advanced years is that, for some, it is the only activity in which engagement is possible.

While there are many written prayers which apply to the experiences of older people, there is one which stands in a class by itself. Though not actually composed by Cardinal Newman, it consists

of phrases which are his and which appeared in two of his sermons. Because of his instinctive sense of English style, Newman
was able to produce phrases which will be remembered as long as
the language exists. His basic figure is that in which he compares
life to a single day, a figure especially appealing to those of advanced years, who love to sing "Abide with me; fast falls the
eventide." The prayer with the haunting Newman phrases is as
follows:

> Support us, O Lord, all the day long, until the shadows lengthen and
> the evening comes, and the busy world is hushed, and the fever of life
> is over and our work is done. Then, in thy mercy grant us a safe lodging
> and a holy rest and peace at the last. Amen.

I do not know how many years I yet have to live; but, however
many or few they may be, I want to lift as many human burdens
as I possibly can. We are always called to serve, but the calling
is even more insistent when the time is short.

The final wisdom about life is epitomized in the words of Christ,
"We must work the works of him who sent me, while it is day;
night comes, when no one can work" (John 9:4, RSV). Here is the
ultimate combination of realism and hope! Since each person
knows that the night will come, though the exact time is beyond
our knowledge, the only reasonable conclusion is to determine to
make the most of the days we still have. There is really nothing
more to say, and nothing more that needs to be said.

DATE			
JUN 10 '82			
APR 6 '83			
April 20			
MY 5 '83			
JUL 1 2 '84			
DE 20 91			
MY 18 '92			

Ⓒ THE BAKER & TAYLOR CO.